LM

Upho

– A Beginn

Upholstery
– A Beginners' Guide

David James

GUILD OF MASTER CRAFTSMAN PUBLICATIONS LTD

First published 2004 by
Guild of Master Craftsman Publications Ltd,
166 High Street, Lewes,
East Sussex BN7 1XU

Reprinted 2004, 2005 (three times)

Text, illustrations and photographs © copyright
David James 2004
Copyright in the Work © Guild of Master Craftsman
Publications Ltd

ISBN 1 86108 276 2

Production Manager: Hilary MacCallum
Managing Editor: Gerrie Purcell
Commissioning Editor: April McCroskie
Editor: Clare Miller
Designer: Ian Hunt

Typeface: Helvetica Neue

Colour origination by Icon Reproduction, London

Printed and bound by Stamford Press, Singapore

Contents

Introduction

Upholstery is a furniture-making craft, but by nature it also includes elements of soft furnishing, woodworking and occasionally some metal work. The upholsterer's principal occupation is to furnish and decorate using a variety of different materials and fabrics and therefore a wide range of skills are required. A chair, for example, can contain a huge range of different materials, from shaped metal to the finest silk, and from modern cellular plastics to fine animal hair, such as cashmere.

The type of work can also be quite varied. An upholsterer may be called upon to cover the walls of a whole room with textiles. Folding screens, stools and ottomans are regular candidates for refurbishment, as is bringing back to life an old armchair or sofa.

A chair frame, which is the starting point for most upholstered seating, may be built from formed ironwork, moulded plastics or strong hardwood timbers. The basis of a piece of upholstered seating is the support or the skeleton, usually referred to as the frame, on to which the upholstery is built and fixed.

There are, however, some notable exceptions, such as the bean-bag, the floor cushion and the pouffe. All these are self-supporting and have little or no conventional inner framework. The diverse range of subject matter is all in a day's work for those who take up upholstery. The work is varied, interesting and very creative.

This book aims to guide you through the basics and introduce you to the possibilities. As your skills develop and you become confident with the tools and materials involved, you will begin to create a style and a method of working that you are comfortable with and can enjoy.

Whether you are learning the craft or simply having a go at some basic refurbishment in the home, a knowledge of the structure of a stool, a chair or a sofa will help you to understand the materials used and how they will react to the upholstery process. The beginner can then judge and compare the problems and also see the possibilities and very often the limitations of a structure.

Furniture construction is a fairly technical business and needs to be precise. Upholstery construction follows a similar pattern but at the same time will allow you to be creative. The pleasure of building something with your hands and then adding a dash of colour with your choice of covering is very satisfying. Equally, trimming and finishing a piece of work with braids, cording tassels and buttons is time-consuming and needs care, but an enormous amount of satisfaction can be gained from completing a piece of work.

It is important to work with sincerity and a sense of curiosity and then gradually find for yourself the way you wish to progress. This may be in modern upholstery, traditional upholstery, pure restoration, or perhaps a happy combination of all these areas.

It is essential that you base your experience on reliable practices. As your interest grows, your enjoyment will increase and you will want to share that interest with others. Find out about the work of other upholsterers and compare their methods and techniques with your own progress.

It is fortunate that the upholstery fixed to any framework can be dismantled, usually in the reverse order that it was assembled in the first place. Assuming that it was done well originally, then, with care, tacks and staples can be lifted and the layers of upholstery removed. Although it is not necessary to copy exactly the upholstery that you find, this will be a good starting point. It will provide a useful background for your reupholstery and a point from which the new work can begin.

Materials, Techniques and Designs

1 Planning

2 Materials

3 Fabrics and trimmings

1 Planning

There is basically very little difference in upholstering a new seating frame compared with an older one. Once the existing upholstery has been removed the older piece will need to be cleaned and any rough timber areas will need smoothing with a fine rasp and some course sandpaper. A new frame does have the advantage of being fresh, clean and ready to use, and work can begin almost immediately. Look out for any very sharp edges on new timber rails and remove them, especially upper inside edges which may come into contact with the new upholstery materials. The wood rasp is an essential part of an upholstery tool kit and will be needed when preparing a new frame as well as an old one.

New or old?

The beginner will of course be able to glean some knowledge of the upholstery process when existing materials are being removed. The exercise of carefully stripping, layer by layer will be quite valuable and informative, although it is only possible if the previous work has been well done or is original and has stood the test of time.

Occasionally some of the old upholstery taken off can be reused and blended with the new. With some experience it will be noticeable that foundation materials, such as webbings, hessian cloths, springs and spring lashing can seldom be reused. It is mainly first and second stuffings of animal hair fillings which are worth cleaning and conserving for reuse. The reuse of old materials is never a short-cut. It takes time to clean and reapply such materials. However, conservation is well worth considering if the furniture deserves that kind of sensitive treatment and you are keen to preserve very old materials of this kind.

At the end of the projects section a set of Louis XVI style salon chairs has been treated in this way and is a good example of how upholstery restoration blends the use of the old and the new.

Before you begin

There are a number of different ways that you can begin to learn about upholstery. If you choose to start with a new wooden frame then it will help if you read through most of this book, so that you have a mental picture of how the work will progress to the finished piece. It is also helpful to find a photograph or a drawing of a similar example to the piece that you are doing. Being faced with a blank stool or chair frame will be rather like starting a journey without a map, or writing an essay without any points of reference.

The wooden frame will tell you a certain amount, but not enough about the depth, scale or proportion to which the upholstery should be built. Over-upholstering or over-stuffing is a common fault and can be avoided with a little planning and thought before you start. Shape and proportion are controlling factors when upholstery is being built so that the end result is neither too thin or too heavy.

Equally the end result needs to be strong, supporting and of course, functional. It is important to be able to visualize the finished work as this will influence the way in which the foundation is made up and in particular your choice of basic materials and method.

In the projects section, different techniques and material choices are illustrated. From these you can select your own treatment to suit the piece you are doing. Reupholstery of an existing chair or stool for example, will begin with taking a photograph of the original. The old upholstery can then be carefully removed, layer by layer, and kept. Keeping the old work in a large plastic bag will firstly provide a useful reference, and secondly make it available for reuse, should this be possible or desirable.

Reupholstery, as opposed to restoration, generally means that the item is in need of complete replacement upholstery. It is a good starting point for the beginner, because a great deal can be learnt by the stripping and removal of an old covering followed by the fillings, lining cloths and a firm or sprung foundation. The seat part of a chair is always the first to suffer from wear and tear, whereas chair arms and back upholstery are much less vulnerable. You may wish to consider at this stage how much replacement of the foundation work is necessary, and plan for part replacement followed by a complete new covering fabric.

The same rules for treatment will apply if you are restoring the upholstery of a very old piece of furniture. There may be a need for complete replacement or part reupholstery before the whole piece is given a new covering.

Upholstery restoration techniques apply mainly to pieces of furniture which are very old and would come under the heading of period or antique or to pieces that have some particular importance. I have outlined how in each of these cases – new work, reupholstery or period – the approach and the treatment will be different.

Frame preparation

On both new and old seating frames there is always some preparation needed before upholstery can begin. All the sharp timber rail edges should be removed using a rasp or some very course sandpaper. Softened edges are much kinder to the new upholstery materials being applied. Chafing and wearing of the webbings and hessian linings will

then be avoided. On an old frame which has been stripped, rough areas and splintered edges caused by stripping should be removed and smoothed down in the same way consolidating by filling where necessary.

Stripping

Removing existing upholstery must be carried out with great care so that damage to the frame is kept to the absolute minimum – this cannot be emphasized enough. Use the ripping chisel and mallet with short sharp taps and a levering action, to lift, rather than drag the tacks out of the rails. Run the chisel as much as possible in the

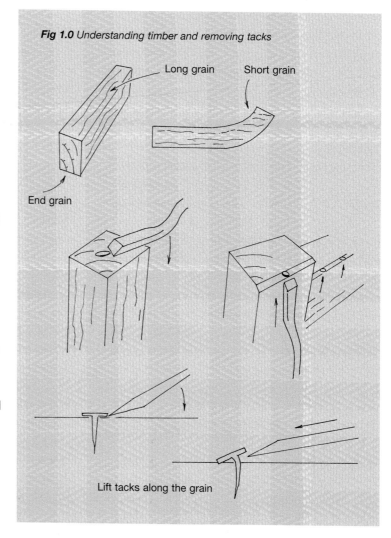

Fig 1.0 *Understanding timber and removing tacks*

Long grain

Short grain

End grain

Lift tacks along the grain

direction of the grain, along the length of the rails, rather than across the grain of the timber, and this will keep splitting down to a minimum, especially when tacks are being lifted close to rail edges. The timber is likely to be dry and quite brittle in many older pieces of furniture (Fig 1.0).

A small pair of pointed snips will help with the removal of tacks, gimp pins and staples once they have been part lifted, especially when removing upholstery close to polished edges and rebates. The corners, for example on show-wood frames, are always vulnerable. Curved and delicate rails particularly, may have short grain at their ends and these will need extra care if breaking is to be avoided. If a break or a large splinter does occur the piece can be glued back and cramped in place once stripping is finished, so make sure that these are kept safely.

The upholstery process can be very demanding on a seat, stool or chair frame. A frame should therefore be in good condition structurally, and able to withstand the early straining when the heavier materials such as webbings, hessians and springs are being built in.

Getting started

Have a look at the gallery of upholstered pieces in chapter 8. There is nothing too large or complicated, but the pieces are quite creative in the way that their details and the coverings can vary so much. You will be able to combine upholstery detail with trimmings and coverings to produce work that makes your upholstery individual and interesting.

You should expect to be able to complete the reupholstery of a loose or drop-in seat (sometimes referred to as a 'slip seat') in a dining chair or side chair, in little more than a day. A pinstuffed seat will take about the same length of time. Both of these types of upholstery are excellent starting projects. Pinstuffed work demands a little more precision when covering, trimming and finishing.

Time taken and what you may expect to achieve will depend on the length of your working sessions. I tend to think of a day in terms of seven to eight hours.

Try to set up an area for working that you can leave and return to later without having to clear away between sessions. Essential items for the work area are a low table about 28in (70cm) high or a pair of low upholstery trestles. Nearby, you will need a side table or some shelving. This provides a resting place for tools and also the enormous amount of small items and sundries that are needed for upholstery work. For example pins, chalk, needles, skewers, threads, tape measure, cords, twines and so on. The list is endless, and the nearer the items are then the less interrupted the work will be.

For your safe working it is advisable to have some or all of the following: a soft leather glove with the finger ends cut off; a dust mask; an apron or smock; a box of finger plasters; some ear-plugs if noise is a problem.

Preparing equipment

Part of the preparation for upholstery is to ensure that you have all the various items needed, tools, sundries, materials, upholstery fabric and trimmings. Other basic equipment will be optional, depending on where you are working and the size and type of your project.

A low table or ideally a pair of upholstery trestles will be needed to support the work at the most comfortable height for you. In addition a side table, a bench, or some shelving is perfect for storing all the small handtools and sundries that will be needed. These all need to be close at hand and easily reached as the work progresses. Some protective clothing is always worth considering as the work can be very dusty and quite physical (Fig 1.1). You may wish to use a dust mask while stripping and removing old upholstery. Wear an apron or smock to protect clothing and use a soft

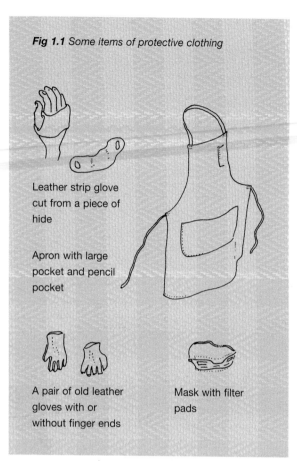

Fig 1.1 *Some items of protective clothing*

Leather strip glove cut from a piece of hide

Apron with large pocket and pencil pocket

A pair of old leather gloves with or without finger ends

Mask with filter pads

leather glove to protect the hand when pulling cords and twines during stitching or lashing.

Upholstery tools and needles are sharp, so you will find that the odd plaster for the fingers may well be needed, especially when you are handling new covering fabrics.

Early on in your work you will want to know how much top covering fabric and trimmings will be required. Upholstery fabrics are sold by the metre and vary in width from 48in to 57in (122cm to 145cm). Measure your piece of work and make generous allowances for pulling and any shaped areas. Upholstery fabrics are applied and fixed with the weft threads running parallel to the floor. Trimmings are also sold by the metre length. Braids, gimps, cords, and fringes are all used to finish edges and to decorate and enhance

upholstery. Pipings and double piping are another option. These are usually made up from the upholstery fabric that is being used.

The hand tools required for upholstery work are relatively inexpensive. Some of the tools used are quite common household items and some are very specialized. The better the range and quality then the better the resulting work will be. It is certainly better to buy in as many as possible and keep your tool kit purely for the upholstery that you do.

Always buy those tools that you feel most comfortable with, keeping them lightweight and easy to handle. This applies particularly to hammers and scissors, because they are the two tools most often used.

Once the work gets under way you will be tacking with the hammer and snipping with the scissors almost continuously. It is essential therefore that both of these are the correct weight and size and you feel happy and comfortable using them.

When you are choosing and purchasing hand tools, buy each tool separately and handle them before deciding. Avoid the pre-packed set of upholstery tools, they are seldom of good quality. Eventually you will want to add to your basic kit and purchase a slightly different hammer and a second pair of shears, either smaller or larger than your first.

Take care of your tools by keeping them together in a tool box or bag. Wrap needles, regulators and knives in a roll of fabric or leather to preserve sharpness and keep them safe – sharp tools present a danger if left lying around.

A small length of emery cloth or a small slip-stone should be part of the kit so that any tool with a point or a blade can be finely tuned and kept at its best for working.

Use the checklist on the right as a guide to the basics that you will need, including some optional power tools.

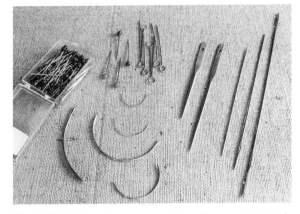

Fig 1.2 *Upholstery skewers, curved needles, regulators and two-point straight needles*

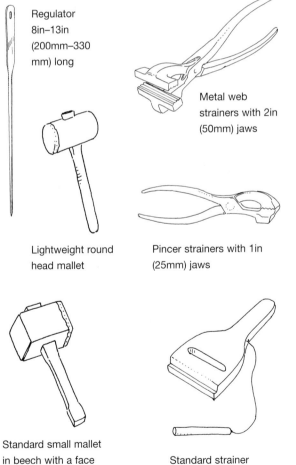

Regulator
8in–13in
(200mm–330 mm) long

Metal web strainers with 2in (50mm) jaws

Lightweight round head mallet

Pincer strainers with 1in (25mm) jaws

Standard small mallet in beech with a face covered in hide

Standard strainer with dowel

Fig 1.3 *Some examples of basic upholstery tools*

Equipment

- Tacking hammer
- Wooden mallet
- Ripping chisel
- Staple lifter
- Upholstery scissors or shears
- Webbing stretcher
- 10in (25cm) and 8in (20cm) two-point needles
- 5in (12½cm) and 3in (7½cm) circular needles
- 6in (15cm) curved springing needle
- 10in (25cm) or 8in (20cm) regulator
- Upholstery skewers (about 30)
- 1¼in (3cm) plated pins
- Pair of pincers and a pair of snips
- Small wood rasp
- Tape measure
- Metre stick or straight edge
- Trimming knife
- Small block of bees wax
- Staple gun, spring loaded, electric or pneumatic
- Use of a sewing machine
- A strip of emery cloth glued onto a small piece of batten, for keeping needles and blades sharp
- Foam saw (or electric bread knife)
- Power drill
- Hot-melt glue gun

2 Materials

We use a wide range of materials for both modern and traditional upholstery. Over the years many materials have been adapted to make them more effective and cheaper to produce, and changes continue to occur.

Use the best materials that can be afforded and that are available to you, this approach will show in your work and help you to produce upholstery of good quality.

The selection of materials and choosing what to use in a particular job is an important part of the upholstery work. Above all, enjoy shopping around for the best and get into the habit of using both natural and synthetic materials where they are best suited to the project you are working on.

Tacks

Tacks are one of the very basic essentials for all kinds of upholstery work. They are used for both temporary and permanent fixing and are blued to keep them clean, distinctive and rust free. However, if they should become exposed to damp for any length of time they will rust.

Upholstery tacks are selected by their size for different uses and generally it is true that the larger sizes are for heavy work, such as fixing hessians, webbings, and lashing cords. The smaller sizes are kept particularly for fixing scrim, calico and upholstery fabrics.

There are two grades of tack, fine and improved, the improved types have a larger head than the fine grade. The different leg lengths are available in both grades. It is not necessary to have all the sizes in both fine and improved, but a useful selection would be: ⅝in (1.5cm) improved, ½in (1.3cm) fine, ⅜in (1cm) fine and ¼in (6mm) fine. These four will be quite adequate for most types of upholstery work. Some 1.3cm (½in) improved could be added to the list as a strong tack for general and light webbing work. 1.5cm (⅝in) improved are used for very heavy fixings and for lashing work with springs and so on. As a general rule, it is a good idea to keep the tack sizes to the smaller grades and sizes wherever possible.

Hammering in large tacks unnecessarily is noisy, tiring and will cause damage, so choose fine tacks in the shorter lengths for most general fixings, and keep the improved and longer lengths for the occasional heavy applications. See figure 2.0 for examples of tack size and suitable spacing.

Gimp pins

A fine-cut steel tack with a very small head which is painted in a variety of different colours. Gimp pins are used as a finishing tack to fix upholstery fabrics and braids or gimps, and as a first fixing before decorative nailing and banding. There are two leg lengths: ⅜in and ½in (1cm and 1.3cm).

Use gimp pins instead of tacks where timber rails are delicate and where decorative edges are to be trimmed. Keep a small stock of both lengths in several different colours. Fawn, black and white are the most common, while red green and blue are also readily available.

Staples

The staple is an alternative fixing used in upholstery and has to be fired into a frame with a stapler or staple gun. The staple is a quick, efficient and clean method of fixing materials to a timber frame. However once fired in, a staple is more difficult to remove than a tack. Staple fixings can be less intrusive and damaging, particularly when a frame is old or delicate and not able to cope with repeated hammering. Ideally use tacks as a temporary fixing and to set linings and covers in place. When shaping and stretching is complete and there is no need for further adjustment, then use the staple as a permanent finish.

Fig 2.0 *Some examples showing the tack size and the adequate tack spacing. Tacks spaced at 1in (2.5cm) provide good strong fixing for most types of work.*

Seldom is there a need to tack any closer, and often a larger space will be quite adequate

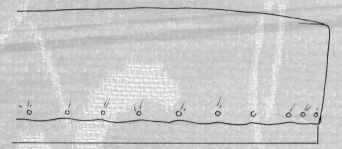

⅜in (1cm) fine tacks 2.5cm (1in) apart for calico

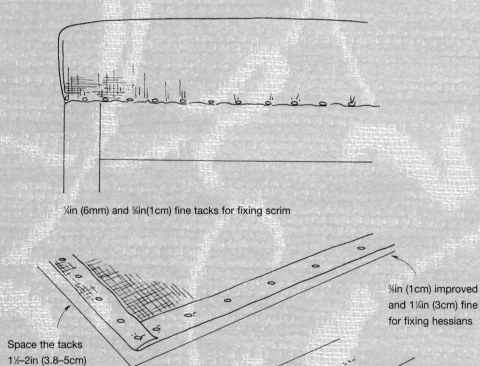

¼in (6mm) and ⅜in(1cm) fine tacks for fixing scrim

⅜in (1cm) improved and 1¼in (3cm) fine for fixing hessians

Space the tacks 1½–2in (3.8–5cm) apart

Use ½in(1.3cm) improved and fine for webbings

Staple sizes

The width of a staple is called the crown width and this may vary from one manufacturer to another. The leg lengths available for upholstery are between ⅛in and ⅝in (3mm and 16mm). Use ⅛–¼in (3–6mm) for fine shallow surfaces, ⅜in (1cm) for most average fixings and ½–⅝in (1.3–1.6cm) for stronger heavy applications, for example when working with webbing.

Webbings

Tightly stretched strips of webbing have been used to support upholstered seating for around 300 years. Basically we still use the same system today even though the raw materials and the structure of webbings has developed and improved in many ways. There are now many variations to suit the different methods of furniture manufacture, and the amount of support, both firm and flexible, required of a chair seat (Fig 2.1).

Nylon, polypropylene, synthetic rubbers, metals, cotton, jute and linen are all used in the making of webbings for upholstery. Webbings for upholstery are mostly 5cm (2in) wide but on the continent they tend to be a little wider, up to 3½in (9cm).

For traditional upholstery work the conventional 5cm (2in) black and white, brown and white and all brown are used. These are all made from natural raw materials, but they often have a small percentage of synthetic fibre added for extra strength.

Modern upholstery has changed and developed dramatically in recent years and webbings, when they are used, are mostly manufactured blends and compositions of materials such as nylon, metals, and rubbers. Products such as elastic webbing, rubber webbing and woven polypropylene webbing are well suited to the design and manufacture of the modern chair.

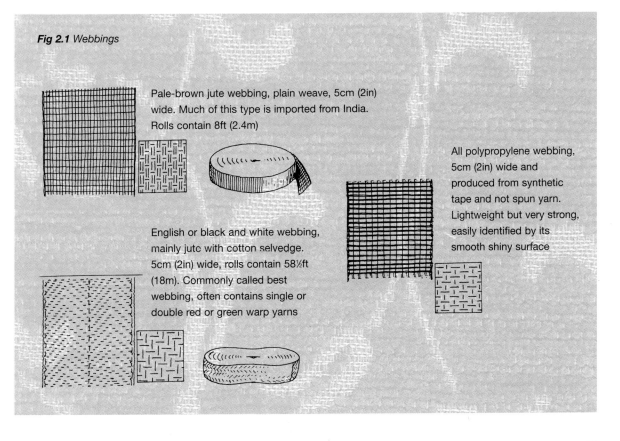

Fig 2.1 *Webbings*

Pale-brown jute webbing, plain weave, 5cm (2in) wide. Much of this type is imported from India. Rolls contain 8ft (2.4m)

All polypropylene webbing, 5cm (2in) wide and produced from synthetic tape and not spun yarn. Lightweight but very strong, easily identified by its smooth shiny surface

English or black and white webbing, mainly jute with cotton selvedge. 5cm (2in) wide, rolls contain 58½ft (18m). Commonly called best webbing, often contains single or double red or green warp yarns

There are two versions of what is known as English webbing, the black and white and the brown and white. These are both excellent and easily available. The alternatives are the 10lb (4.5kg) and 12lb (5.5kg) all brown webs, made from 100% jute and sold in their natural colours. The two types, English and Jute are distinguished by their weave patterns, which are herringbone twill and plain weave.

Black bottom linings

Another fine plain woven lining cloth, usually dyed black and used as a finishing cover or dust cover on the underside of chairs and settees. As the name suggests a bottom lining is used to provide a neat finish and a dust cover under seats. The edges of the lining are always turned in and neatly tacked or stapled along the centre of the rails, and never too near to the outer edge. Black linings are functional and should never be seen. A 10oz (305g) hessian can also be used as an under-cover when a black cloth is not available. Occasionally a lining of this type is used to line a seat by fixing it on top of the rails before upholstery begins. This type of finish is well suited to small unsprung occasional chairs and dining chairs.

Calico

A fine white, unbleached cotton cloth used in upholstery as a lining or first covering over second stuffings. It is good practice to complete a piece of upholstery in calico, before the final or top cover is applied. A calico lining can be very tightly stretched and allows precise shaping, so that upholstery fabrics, which may sometimes be delicate, can be pulled down and fixed with care. Calico will take much of the initial strain and will also support the top covering, giving it a good appearance and at the same time prolonging it's life. A calico lining will also allow the beginner to experiment and to test difficult cutting operations at corners and around frame supports, legs, arms and so on.

Once a calico cover is in place it can be used as a marking surface where features and details are to be built into the upholstery design, for example, pull-ins, tufting and shallow fluting. Collars around arms and piped joints can also be accurately positioned and drawn before the main covering stage. Calico covers are seldom turned in at their edges, but are simply pulled down and tacked on to rail faces before being trimmed close to the tack line.

Cambric

A fine close-weave all-cotton fabric with a very smooth surface, which is usually glazed. Cambric is an excellent lining cloth that is made feather-proof by a waxing process. It has a luxurious feel and is used principally as a cushion interior lining for feather and down fillings.

The cloth works well and can be cut and sewn with good accuracy. Available in 36in (90cm), 48in (122cm) and 72in (180cm) widths. When making up cambric into cushion cases, the shiny side of the cloth should be to the inside or filling side to help the movement of the fillings.

Ticking

Ticking is a strong twill weave fabric, traditionally woven from white cotton with a narrow black stripe in the warp direction. It is proof against fibrous filling materials such as feathers, hair, flocks and kapok. Tickings are available in a variety of widths and are also produced as soft furnishing fabrics in both colour stripe and woven patterns for bedding and upholstery.

Duck

A heavyweight version of calico usually 10oz or 15oz (305gm and 458gm). Cotton duck is used as a support material in modern upholstery and in outdoor seating, such as deckchairs. It cuts and works well and is generally plain weave. Available in 39in (1m), 59in (1½m) and 79in (2m) widths.

Stockinette

A single jersey knitted fabric made from rayon and other synthetic yarns. Stockinette is made in a continuous sock and will stretch to several times its relaxed size.

A length of stockinette is cut from the roll and stretched over foams, cushion interiors and synthetic fibre fillings. It is basically a very soft lightweight lining used to contain and hold in place, and make handling easier.

Use stockinette linings over foams and foam/fibre interiors, before covering with upholstery fabric. The cut ends are sealed by hand stitching, overlocking or heat sealing.

Upholstery scrim

Scrim cloths are used for shaping work over first stuffings in traditional upholstery. They can be easily manipulated and are generally finer in weave and yarn than a hessian. Jute yarns are used to weave and produce 6oz (185gm) and 9oz (290gm) hessian scrims, 180cm (72in) wide.

Linen scrims are made from 100% linen (flax) yarns and are considered to be the best for fine shape work and edge making in upholstery. However, they are noticeably more expensive and are only available in 90cm (36in) widths. For general edge work a 9oz (290gm) hessian scrim gives a very satisfactory result.

Hessian

A strong, course plain woven cloth made from 100% jute and used in upholstery as a supporting base cloth. Hessians are bought by the metre length and are available in several different widths, for example, 30in (76cm), 36in (90cm), 101.6cm (40in), 157.4cm (72in). The quality of a hessian is measured by the weight of a square metre in ounces or grams. Typical weights for upholstery work are: 7½oz (229gm), 10oz (305gm), 12oz (366gm), 15oz (458gm).

10oz (305gm) hessian is a medium weight and is ideal for general lining work. 12oz (366gm) is recommended as a minimum weight over sprung upholstery in backs and seats. A large fully sprung seat should be lined with 15oz (452gm) hessian (sometimes referred to as tarpaulin).

Twines and cords

Strong twines and cord are used for tying, stitching and lashing in all kinds of upholstery work. Mattress twines, as they are called, are used for all types of stitch work, and are made from pure linen. Twine numbers 3, 4 and 5 are the thicknesses most used in traditional work. No 3 is ideal for edge stitching and the heavier No 5 for the more general tying and stitching.

Lashing cords, called laid cords, are the very strong heavy cords used to lash and hold springs in place, in chair seats and backs. Made from hemp, laid cords are designed specifically to do a tough job and remain stable under tension.

Slipping threads

A strong linen stitching thread used for the hand stitching and closing of upholstery covering fabrics. These threads are bought in skeins or small reels in a variety of different colours. Keep a stock of a few colours. Your selection should include, 'drab' (a muddy brown), black and some white. When slip stitching, the thread is virtually invisible, and so drab will do for use with most fabric colours. However, an additional small

Fig 2.2 A selection of plaited slipping thread

selection of colours will always ensure that you are able to get the nearest possible match.

Slipping threads are lightly waxed which keeps them strong, twist free, and gives the thread good grip in order to produce a tight and positive hand-made join.

Springs and flexible webbings

The springs used for traditional upholstery are double cone compression springs. They are waisted at their centres and have an hourglass shape. There is a good range of sizes available from 7.5cm (3in) up to 22.9cm (9in) high and with wire gauges or thicknesses (swg) from 14swg down to 8swg. The higher the gauge number then the finer the wire will be, and so the softer the spring will be.

Spring wires used for seats tend to be from 8swg up to 10swg, and those used in chair-back supports and chair-arm upholstery will generally be in the range 11 to 14swg wires. Some seat springs are available in half sizes, for example, 9½swg and 10½swg. Below are some spring sizes and some recommended uses for each.

4in (10cm) x 9swg	for stools and firm chair-seat platforms, under cushions.
5in (12.5cm) x 9½swg	for firm chair seats and fully sprung arm chairs.
5in (12.5cm) x 9swg	as above.
6in (15cm) x 9½swg	for easy chairs and wing chairs, nursing chairs and sewing chairs.
6in (15cm) x 10swg	for fully sprung arm chairs and spring edge seats.

Tension springs

Tension springs are a very different type of upholstery spring, designed for use in the modern chair. These were first introduced in the 1950s in

Fig 2.3 The double cone upholstery spring, sold in bundles of fifty

seating and were well suited to the more lightweight, less deep-upholstered chairs of the time. The close-coiled cable spring and the zig-zag wire spring are both tension springs and have been used in large quantities during the second half of the 20th century. They are both used as lateral suspension and are stretched under tension across a chair seat or back frame.

Flexible webbings

Available as rubber webbings or as elastic webbings with various proprietary fixings. Both of these flexible webbings are available in roll lengths that can be fixed and cut as desired onto chair frames. Depending on the type of webbing chosen, tensioning may be from as low as 7½% or as high as 90%. Providing coverage is at around 50% of the area to be sprung – the gap between the webs is equal to the width of the webbing – then these types of webbing produce a very good suspension for modern chair seats and backs. They are also very well suited to both timber and tubular steel frame constructions.

Edge roll and dug roll

Edge rolls are available in ready-to-use form, with or without a flange for fixing. Sizes range from 1cm (⅜in) up to 3cm (1⅛in) diameter. This handy product is used to upholster along seat, arm and

Fillings

Coir (coconut)	ginger and dyed	1st stuffings
Hair	grey curled hair	1st and 2nd stuffings
	white combings	1st and 2nd stuffings
	horse hair	1st and 2nd stuffings
	cashmere	2nd stuffings
Flax	undyed	1st stuffings
Skin wadding	cotton	top stuffings
Polyester wadding	Dacron or Terylene	toppings
Cotton felt		2nd stuffing and topping
Wool felt		2nd stuffing and topping
Rubberized hair	sheet	soft 1st stuffings
Foams	sheet	general

chair-back rail edges, where a quickly applied soft roll is required. It eliminates the need for a more complex edging, more usual in traditional work. Edge roll or dug roll is generally made from recycled paper or a firm extruded plastic foam, and can be cut, stapled or tacked, either directly on to a chair frame, or neatly rolled up into a hessian lining cloth.

Fillings

(See table, above) Coir or coconut fibre is bought as black-dyed or undyed ginger fibre and sold by the kilogramme or pound. This is an ideal filling for use as a first stuffing in traditional upholstery, particularly where a stitched edge is to be built in sprung or unsprung seating. An excellent vegetable filling which has been curled during processing and usually made fire retardant.

Animal hair

Certainly one of the best and most versatile upholstery fillings which has its uses in both traditional and modern upholstery and bedding. Curled animal hair is resilient, warm and inherently fire resistant.

Hair fillings are available in various grades and types. Grey curled hair is the most popular and is a blend of pig, cow and horse mane and tail. White combings from cow-tails is another good grade and is often superior in length and curl, though it is a little more expensive than the grey variety.

Pure horse hair is still available as a superior quality filling. It is chosen for its excellent curl, resilience and length. It is usually imported from France or China and is generally the most expensive of the hair fillings.

Polyester wadding

Available in several thicknesses or weights and in a number of different widths. These waddings are resilient, soft and warm and are used in all kinds of upholstered surfaces. A roll of 162ft (50m) 27in (68cm) wide in 2oz (70g) or 4oz (135g) weight is ideal stock for most applications. It is easily cut, laminated, rolled or folded to any thickness and can be glued or stapled in place when necessary. The resilience and flexibility of polyester waddings make them the upholsterer's best friend. They provide good support and good stretch around curving surfaces, as well as immediately under covering fabrics.

They are now used universally over all foam fillings to provide a soft flexible barrier between foam and fabric covering. Two ounce (70g) wadding has a thickness of about 6mm (¼in) and can be stretched by about 30% in any direction without breaking. This feature makes it ideal as an upholstery medium and will help to produce a good line and a warm soft feel to a surface covering.

Skin wadding

Used very extensively in traditional work as a topping or final stuffing layer, either before calico covering or after, or both. The paper-like surface acts as a barrier that prevents hair fillings from penetrating through linings and covers.

Fig 2.4 Polyester fibre, cotton felt and skin wadding

Skin waddings are purchased in small rolls of 10 or 20 metre lengths which are 457mm (18in) wide. The wadding can be split or opened by parting the thickness to give a very thin layer 914mm (36in) wide. When split, several layers are used together to form a good hair-proof topping.

These waddings are very versatile and can be used layered up to various thicknesses, rolled or folded for borders or for fluting work. The outside coverings on chairs, sofas and so on are usually lined with skin waddings.

Cashmere

A fine goat hair which makes an excellent second stuffing for high-quality traditional upholstery. Cashmere is normally bought as a hair-pad needled into a hessian base, and is sold by the roll or per metre. The hair can easily be pulled out and separated from its hessian cloth base and then teased ready for use as a loose filling.

Its high cost usually means that it tends to be reserved for work of the highest quality, for example, period chairs with unsprung seats and delicate chair-back panels. It is also ideal as a top stuffing in hair-filled squabs and cushions.

Rubberized hair

This is a processed filling bought in sheet form ready for use. Sheets are usually 1in (2.5cm) thick and measure about 78in x 39in (2m x 1m). A very useful and adaptable filling made from a blend of grey curled hair and rubber compounds.

Rubberized hair can be cut easily with scissors, shaped and chamfered, or layered and laminated to various thicknesses required. It bonds well with spray adhesive and can also be fixed in place with tacks and staples. It has good resilience and is ideal for use in bed head-boards and chair-backs and arms as a first stuffing with a thin layer of loose hair and some cotton or wool felt over as a topping.

When laminated up to 5cm (2in) or 7.5cm (3in) thick rubberized hair is an excellent base filling for attaching deep buttoning to, particularly in combination with an overlay or topping of white cotton felt.

Cotton felt and wool felt

As the name suggests these soft fillings are much heavier and thicker than waddings. New cotton and reclaimed wool are felted into useable fillings in roll form, about 2.5cm (1in) thickness. A roll contains around 20 metres which is normally 68cm (27in) wide.

There are two weights or thicknesses available, 2½oz (83g) and 4oz (135g) per square foot. Cotton felts are made from pure new cotton and are a little more expensive than the wool felts, but well worth the extra cost.

Both of these fillings are supported on soft paper which is removed as the felt is unrolled and applied. The paper separates the layers and also facilitates handling. Felts can be torn across the roll width but need to be cut along their length. Edges can be feathered to assist with shaping, by picking and thinning.

Upholstery foams

A cellular plastic upholstery filling which is made from polyurethane, an oil-based product. Foams can be purchased in sheet form at any thickness from 6mm (¼in) up to 10cm (4in). Alternatively, foams are cut and supplied in cushion-size shapes to almost any dimension required. A pattern or template will be needed for shapes or profiles that have varying thickness. At thicknesses above 20cm (8in), large pieces of foam are referred to as blocks. For example, a block or a cube 20in x 20in x 12in (51cm x 51cm x 30cm) can be cut and supplied to those measurements or, a circular block 20in radius x 12in (51cm x 30cm) will require a template as a cutting guide.

Upholstery foams are produced combustion modified (CM) to various densities and hardness. High-density foams are the most expensive and

can be made in a range of different hardnesses. The hardness of a foam is usually referred to as 'the feel'. Here are some typical foam types and their recommended uses. Most foam manufacturers and suppliers will recommend the most suitable for a particular end use.

CM	Combustion modified or fire retardent to different levels or specifications. e.g. domestic use or public use
HR	High resilience
CHIPFOAM	Reconstituted CM foam
PU	Polyurethane
PE	Polyether (conventional foam)

Examples:

Grade	Colour	Density range	Hardness range	Class of use
CMHR25s	White	23–26	50–75	A
CMHR35	Green	38–42	115–150	S
CMHR40h	Blue	38–42	155–190	S
CMHR50	White	48–52	195–235	V

Foam classification (class of use) is the performance of the foam under load-bearing conditions.

Class	Type of class	Recommended application
X	Extremely severe	Heavy duty seating
V	Very severe	Commercial vehicle seats
S	Severe	Domestic seats and mattresses
A	Average	Chair backs and arm rests
L	Light	Padding, cushions, pillows

3 Fabrics and trimmings

The upholsterer uses a very wide range of materials for both traditional and modern work. Many of the materials one would expect to find in a chair made a hundred years ago have of course changed or been replaced – improvements in processing and the introduction of synthetics and new technology make this inevitable. But there is still a considerable demand for many of the good, naturally based materials such as webbings, fillings of animal or vegetable fibre, and woven cloths. Many of these materials have been modified, or their construction changed to improve strength or to make them easier to handle and to use.

Fabrics and trimmings

If you take a close look at a roll of upholstery fabric, and then take a tape measure and check the width of the roll, that is, from one selvedge across to the other, it will be somewhere between 51in and 57in (130cm and 145cm). This is about average and is a very familiar width to anyone buying and using fabrics for upholstery.

The width of a fabric is set by the manufacturing process of weaving. A fabric is created by weaving two basic sets of yarns together, the weft yarns, which are those running across or side to side, and the warp yarns, which are those running down the length of the fabric, or the roll. These fabrics are bought by the metre, and once cut, they are referred to as cut lengths.

Furnishing fabrics are generally grouped into three categories; curtaining, loose covers and fixed upholstery. Those made for upholstery will mainly be more robust and heavier in weight. They need to be fit for the purpose and be capable of

being cut and sewn, stretched and fixed, as well as having good resistance to wear and tear.

Today we demand clear information about the products that we buy and fabrics are no exception. Look for the labelling on a fabric and check the fibre content, the width of the fabric in centimetres, it's suitability for use, the colourways available, the pattern repeat size, and of course, the price per metre.

Ask for as much information as possible about the fabric that you intend to buy and always buy just a little more than you actually need. As soon as possible after purchase check the fabric closely yourself, making sure that it is the length that you intended, the condition is good and there are no surface faults. Most suppliers will be happy to replace a faulty piece, providing you have not cut into it, and that you have the original receipt.

There are a vast range of light, medium and heavy coverings which are eminently suitable for upholstery use. A large percentage of these contain natural fibres which are frequently blended

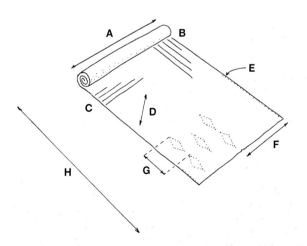

A Width
B Warp yarns
C Weft yarns
D Bias direction
E Selvedge
F Half width
G Pattern repeat
H Length or cut length

Fig 3.0 A Typical upholstery cover/fabric

with synthetics to create the properties required for the job. Wool, cotton and linen are often blended with rayon, nylon or acrylics to give the best of both worlds.

Over the long history of the upholstery textile, styles, colourings and textures have changed, developed, and moved in and out of fashion. Below is an interesting sample of the varieties that have been used to furnish chairs and sofas since the beginning of the 17th century.

Early 17th century;	Indian cottons, Turkish work, plain wool cloths
Late 17th century;	velvets, silk brocade, leathers
Early 18th century	embroidery work, damask, chintz
Late 18th century;	French and English tapestry, haircloth
Early 19th century;	brocades, silk damask, patterned velour
Late 19th century;	wool plush, embossed leather, printed cottons
Early 20th century	leathercloths, printed unions, stylized tapestry
Late 20th century	moquette, tweeds, synthetic velvets, chenille

Taking care of your upholstery fabrics

Whenever possible avoid folding a fabric or a leather, either before or after cutting. Large or small pieces should be rolled and laid on a flat surface if left for any length of time. Velvets, hides and leathercloths are particularly vulnerable to permanent creasing by folding.

The fabric on a piece of upholstered furniture is usually the most expensive part and may well exceed the value of all the other materials. Use a dust cover when work is not in progress on a piece of work that is partially covered with fabric or completed.

Regular soft brushing or gentle vacuum cleaning will keep covers in good condition. Fabrics are weakened by dust and grit. Most fabric suppliers grade their range of covers for wear. The wearing qualities of upholstery fabrics vary enormously, depending on the strength of the yarn and the weaving technique used. Pile fabrics such as velvet and chenille may flatten when people sit on them. This is mostly inevitable and does not affect the durability of the fabric.

Leather will age and crease attractively but will need cleaning from time to time. Leather suppliers will be happy to advise about cleaning but basically, after removing dust the surface should simply be wiped with a cloth that has been dampened with a very mild soap.

Whenever possible cushions should be plumped and rotated to keep furniture looking fresh and good and to spread the wear. Fabrics are damaged by direct heat and strong sunlight, which weakens fibres and fades the colours. Loose threads should never be cut or pulled but carefully threaded and needled back into the upholstery.

Spillages and stains need to be dealt with quickly, but don't use anything wetter than a damp cloth. Soaking an upholstery fabric can leave a permanent mark or cause puckering and damage to the interior.

Choosing and using furnishing fabrics is an exciting part of the craft of upholstery. An ordinary and very plain piece can be made to look extremely impressive when a good fabric of the right colour with an interesting texture is used. However if a chair, sofa, or screen, for example, has a strong style or is heavily carved, then a relatively plain fabric used for the upholstery will enhance the design.

You will enjoy the freedom to work with fabrics and coverings in both a functional and a decorative way. Techniques such as pleating, ruching and buttoning are widely used and have become recognized work methods based on historic development. Each in its way produces the surface detail and design that gives a piece of upholstered furniture its distinct style or finish.

Many of these decorative techniques are simply fine details used to trim and enhance as expressions of the craft. You should allow yourself to be influenced by the origin of a piece, or by a desire to simplify or enhance an original style. Although much of the work we do is concerned with chairs and seating of various kinds, the opportunity is always there to use other techniques. Wall coverings, upholstered screens, ottomans and bed upholstery are good examples of how inventive fabric work and trimming methods can produce fascinating results.

Measuring and estimating fabric quantities

Use a tape measure to obtain the length and width of all the fabric parts that you will need. Label the parts and record a set of measurements for each piece of fabric. Assume that the fabric width will be average, for example, 124.5cm to 140cm (49in to 55in), unless you already have the fabric to hand. Draw a sketch plan and lay out all the cover parts onto your plan of the cover.

If the larger parts, such as the inside back or the seat panel, are wider than half the width of the fabric, then it is likely that the next piece in the layout will have to be cut from below, rather than at the side of the first. Always centre the main pieces to be cut by cutting a notch or by putting in a pin and aligning these with the centre of any pattern or stripe. Remember that inside back pieces, outside back pieces and seats on chairs, have to match up and have the same centre line.

Most of the smaller parts where two are required, such as arm pads or facings, can be cut as pairs, which simply means that they will be mirror images, and in most cases will be identical.

Plain coverings are generally easier to deal with and are usually more economical to use. Pile fabrics, such as velvets or velours, although they are plain in appearance, have their own set of rules for cutting. They have a pile surface which has a lay or a nap, and this will make the fabric appear dark when viewed from one direction and much lighter when viewed from another. This is often referred to as shading. When pile fabrics are cut and placed on to a chair, the pile should always brush down and feel smooth. A chair seat will follow on from the back and will brush forward, feeling smooth to the touch when the hand or fingers are brushed from the back of the seat towards the front. All these points have to be considered when fabrics are being chosen, and when they are being cut and prepared to be used for upholstery.

Another useful tip is that all upholstery fabrics are positioned and fixed on to a chair with the weft yarns (horizontal yarns) running parallel to the floor. This applies equally to all the different parts and on any design of chair. Two notable exceptions are railroaded fabrics and horse hair fabrics.

However, the majority of upholstery fabrics are designed and made in the conventional way. That is, the warp yarns run vertically and are the main structure of the fabric, and the weft yarns, running horizontally, form the pattern and the surface texture.

When measurements are recorded before cover cutting, always try to write the length measurement first, followed by the width.

When a sketch plan is completed and all the parts required are drawn, the length measurements can then be totalled to give the overall requirement in metres. Whenever possible the quantity is rounded up to the nearest whole metre. If a fabric has a large pattern or motif the length of the pattern repeat is also added to the total. This helps to ensure that enough of the pattern design is available for the whole project.

A certain amount of waste is inevitable when upholstery fabrics are being cut, however, many of the waste pieces will be used up for smaller parts and also for pipings, fly pieces and sometimes buttons.

4 Basic upholstery techniques

From the middle of the 17th century the upholstery of chairs and seating, as well as occasional furniture and bedding, took on a more structured form. The building and filling of padded areas to provide comfort slowly developed into the craft that we now know as upholstery. Contributions and influences from European craftsmen gradually changed the way in which various natural materials and fillings were used and shaped to produce what is known as stitched-edge upholstery (Figs 4.0 and 4.1).

These basic skills and techniques, which have been handed down for generations, provide us with an essential grounding in the art of upholstery. They need to be practised and repeated, so that a series of skills and a basic knowledge is at your command. This chapter can be used as a reference and a useful reminder as you deal with each different project that needs new upholstery or reupholstery.

Watching an upholsterer at work, whenever there is an opportunity, is another valuable way in which the basics can be appreciated. A great deal can also be learned from dismantling old pieces of upholstered furniture, providing that it is done with care and in the correct sequence. This is a good opportunity to make some notes and take photographs as a reminder of the order of assembly.

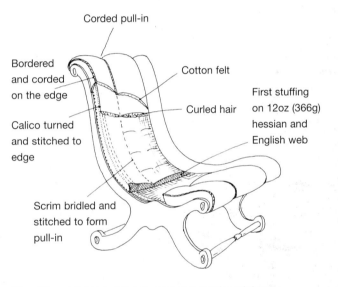

Corded pull-in

Bordered and corded on the edge

Cotton felt

First stuffing on 12oz (366g) hessian and English web

Curled hair

Calico turned and stitched to edge

Scrim bridled and stitched to form pull-in

Figs 4.0 and **4.1** *Upholsterers used and developed these techniques to build and shape loose fillings in order to make up fixed upholstery pads, roll edges, loose squabs, cushions and mattresses.*

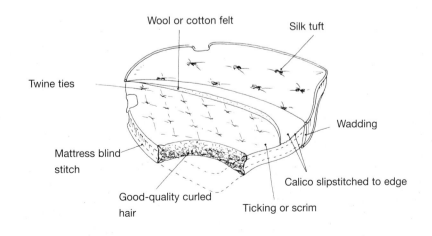

Wool or cotton felt

Silk tuft

Twine ties

Wadding

Mattress blind stitch

Calico slipstitched to edge

Good-quality curled hair

Ticking or scrim

Webs and webbing

Webbings are the materials that are used to support most types of basic upholstery. These are fixed using a web strainer or stretcher, to produce a well-tensioned base.

Figure 4.3 shows some different treatments and variations of webbing patterns. The different patterns are chosen to suit different frame sizes and shapes. For example a seat with curving rails will have a different weave arrangement to a seat with normal straight rails. Similarly, a chair or stool with a round seat frame can be given a different layout or treatment to a seat with a square frame. There are many variations and the more pieces of upholstery that you discover, the more experience will be gained.

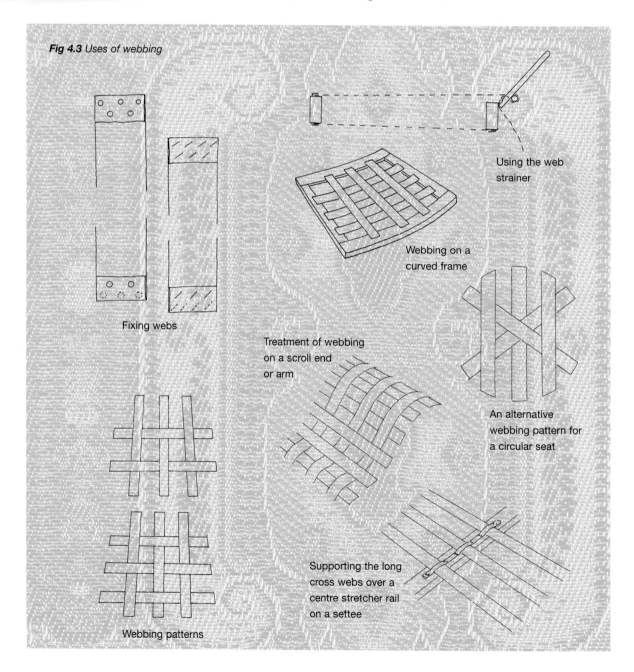

Fig 4.3 *Uses of webbing*

Using the web strainer

Webbing on a curved frame

Fixing webs

Treatment of webbing on a scroll end or arm

An alternative webbing pattern for a circular seat

Supporting the long cross webs over a centre stretcher rail on a settee

Webbing patterns

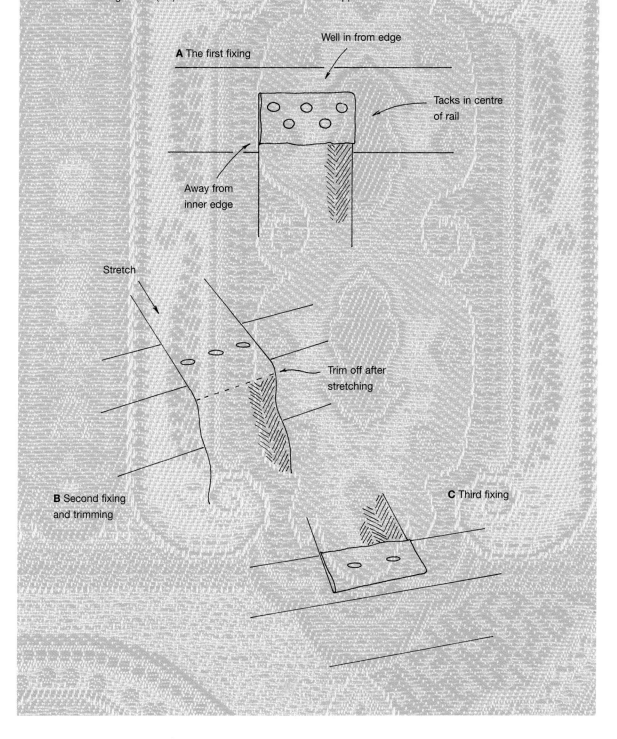

Fig 4.5 *The basic web fixing method is shown below.*
A fold and tack at rail centre using a three and two formation
B stretch the webbing tightly and fit three tacks while under tension
C trim off leaving 20mm (¾in) that is turned back and two tacks applied

A The first fixing

Well in from edge

Tacks in centre
of rail

Away from
inner edge

Stretch

Trim off after
stretching

B Second fixing
and trimming

C Third fixing

It is better to use too much webbing than not enough, and spacing of the webbing should at least be adequate for the job that it will perform. A good general formula that will suit most types of work is to fix webs at 12.5cm (5in) centres, or in the case of seats, where most strain is likely, fix the webbing with spaces equal to the width of the webbing, for example 5cm (2in).

Other than in very lightweight work, a minimum tack size of 1.3cm (½in) fine or improved should be used. Where stapling is preferred then 1.3cm x 1cm (½in and ⅜in) should be used for fixing, the longer staple being used for frames where the timber is old and already full of tack holes.

Lining up in hessian

Hessian is the first covering over webbing where a piece of work is simply top-stuffed and is unsprung. In this case the hessian used is 10oz (305g) or 12oz (366g) weight and is pulled taut by hand tightly in all directions, 1cm (⅜in) fine or improved tacks are used in most cases. Loose seats, top-stuffed seats, arms and wings are lined with hessian in this way (Fig 4.6).

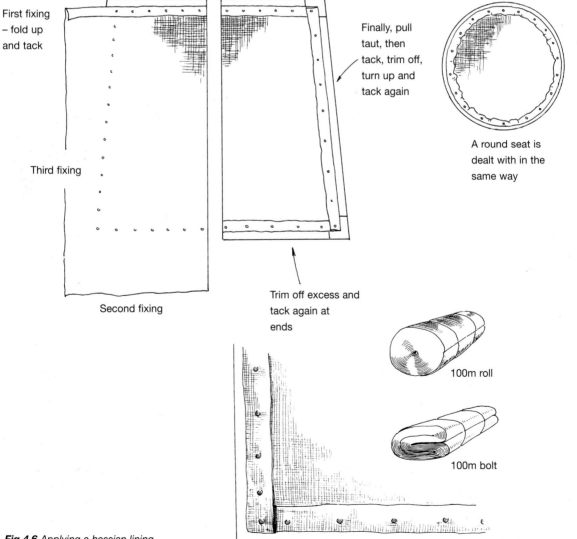

First fixing – fold up and tack

Third fixing

Second fixing

Finally, pull taut, then tack, trim off, turn up and tack again

A round seat is dealt with in the same way

Trim off excess and tack again at ends

100m roll

100m bolt

Fig 4.6 *Applying a hessian lining*

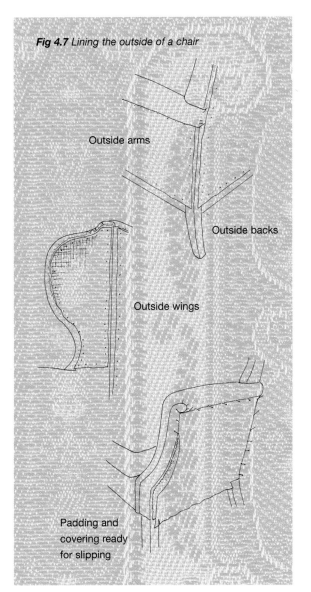

Fig 4.7 Lining the outside of a chair

Outside arms

Outside backs

Outside wings

Padding and
covering ready
for slipping

Knots and twines

Upholstery twines are relatively fine and are
graded as sizes 1 to 5, size number 1 being the
finest. Size number 5 is a heavy twine used
principally for tying in springs and some
lightweight lashing work, and also for buttoning.
Size number 3 is a good weight for stitching and
the forming of stitched edges. When an
exceptionally strong twine is needed for tufting
and buttoning then a yellow nylon twine can be
used, especially where there is likely to be
movement or strain (Fig 4.8).

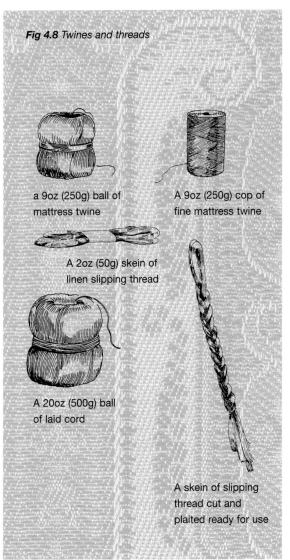

Fig 4.8 Twines and threads

a 9oz (250g) ball of
mattress twine

A 9oz (250g) cop of
fine mattress twine

A 2oz (50g) skein of
linen slipping thread

A 20oz (500g) ball
of laid cord

A skein of slipping
thread cut and
plaited ready for use

When a seat or sometimes a chair back is sprung
then the hessian lining follows after the springs
have been fitted. A 12oz (366g) or tarpaulin-
weight hessian is used over spring work, because
of the extra amount of movement and wear and
tear that is likely in a sprung foundation.

Lightweight hessians such as 7oz (216g) and
10oz (305g) are adequate for lining up the outside
areas of chairs. These support coverings and
waddings when, for example, outside upholstery
fabrics are being applied and finished off (Fig 4.7).

Best-quality flax twines are widely accepted as strong and durable for upholstery work. Upholstery mattress twines as they are bought, may be strengthened and made more durable by the addition of oils and waxes. Many upholsterers who do a lot of stitch work keep a lump of bees wax, through which twine is drawn before use. This will improve the natural strength, help to take out some of the twist and will allow a certain amount of grip on other materials. A non-slip twine makes for good tight positive stitching that holds its shape well.

Most knots and stitches in upholstery are used to join and hold materials together. Many, however, are used to create shape and to build and hold a shaped piece of work in place. Making shapes with loose fillings is a form of sculpture, with the knots and stitches holding and supporting the basic medium to give shape and design to the upholstery.

Everyone working in upholstery uses the slipknot, so much so that it would be difficult to cope without it. The slipknot may be single or double and is adjustable until locked off with a hitch (Figs 4.9 and 4.10). Use a slipknot when starting off bridling, stuffing ties and stitched edges, and for button tying and tufting. The more a slipknot is pulled the tighter it becomes. Use a double slipknot for buttoning and particularly when beginning stitched edge work.

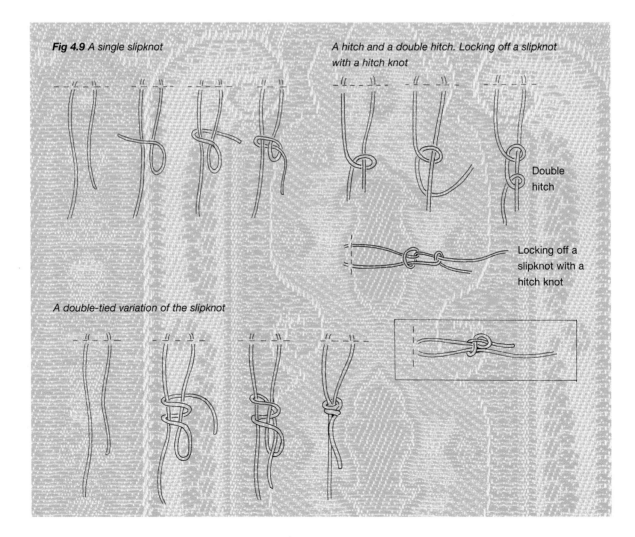

Fig 4.9 A single slipknot

A hitch and a double hitch. Locking off a slipknot with a hitch knot

Double hitch

Locking off a slipknot with a hitch knot

A double-tied variation of the slipknot

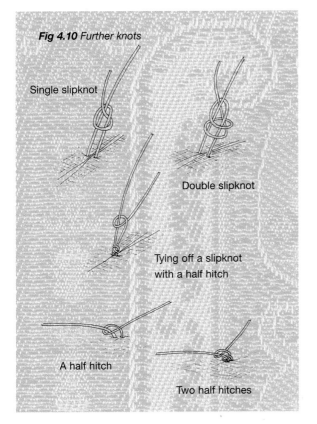

Fig 4.10 Further knots

Single slipknot

Double slipknot

Tying off a slipknot
with a half hitch

A half hitch

Two half hitches

Bridling and tying in the stuffing

All loose stuffings in upholstery work are tied in with ties of twine (Fig 4.11). The ties are stitched into the hessian with a 12.5cm (5in) curved needle or a springing needle. Where stuffings are applied directly on to timber then the ties are tacked down and left as raised loops. This occurs, for example, on arm tops and arm pads. Loose fillings such as curled hair, flocks and coir fibre are pushed under the ties in small handfuls to build an even, resilient padding. As the filling thickens it must be teased out with the fingers to make it even and free from any lumps. Applying fillings to a large area can be tiring work, but creating an even layer is essential. The more the stuffing is worked and teased the better will be the finished results.

It is good practice to run stuffing ties vertically on chair arms and inside backs, as this will lessen the likelihood of fillings slipping down at some time in the future. The bridling of fillings is important and allows the density of the fillings to be controlled. The more the filling is pushed under

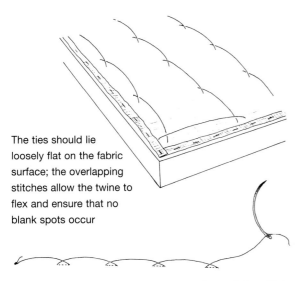

The ties should lie loosely flat on the fabric surface; the overlapping stitches allow the twine to flex and ensure that no blank spots occur

Stuffing ties formed by backstitching at about 12.5cm (5in) spaces

Stuffing ties tacked down onto a wooden frame

Layout of ties on an inside back to help prevent fillings slipping down

An alternative layout for a seat

Layout of ties on a border

Fig 4.11 Stuffing ties

the ties, the more dense and compacted the build can be, and the tighter the loops of twine will become.

First stuffings or foundations

A first stuffing is the foundation of a piece of upholstery supported by the webbings, springs and so on. It needs to be resilient and fairly course in nature, as well as having the ability to be shaped and moulded to conform to the upholstery requirements and the frame design. Good-quality high-density foams are the normal choice for a piece of new modern work, such as 6lb (2.7kg) chipfoams or 40 grade and above in the urethane foam range. Loose traditional fillings such as coir fibre, flax grass and curled hair are all good choices for first stuffings.

Having chosen the most suitable filling, it then needs to be applied until it is a good density, depending of course, on the type of edge to be built (Fig 4.12).

Using scrim

Upholstery scrim is an interesting and extremely useful material, it allows you to shape and form the line of an upholstered edge. Seats, backs and arms of upholstered chairs are covered in scrim after the first stuffing. Scrim is a relatively fine cloth, made from linen or jute and is an essential item in the building of depth and shape in all types of basic upholstery (Figs 4.13 and 4.14). It works well and has a natural strength and flexibility. It would be unusual to find scrim used in a modern chair where foams are the predominant filling, but for any traditional work a good scrim provides the first covering over loose fibrous fillings, held in place with ties of twine, while edges are formed on squabs, cushions and fixed-chair work. Scrim is one of the few materials in upholstery that are turned in and tacked. Most other materials are turned out at their edges or tacked down and trimmed off, leaving a raw cut edge. For best results, use a pure linen scrim or a 9oz (290g) jute

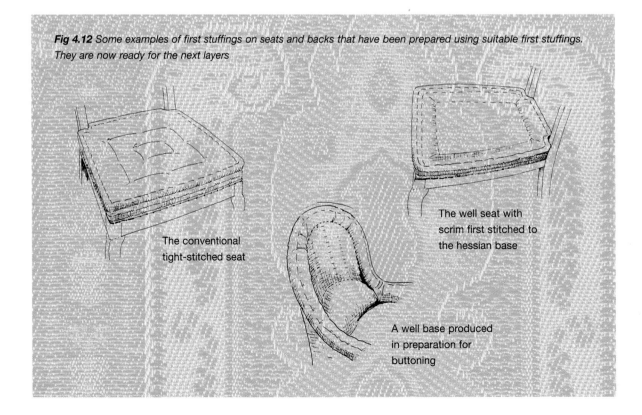

Fig 4.12 *Some examples of first stuffings on seats and backs that have been prepared using suitable first stuffings. They are now ready for the next layers*

The conventional tight-stitched seat

The well seat with scrim first stitched to the hessian base

A well base produced in preparation for buttoning

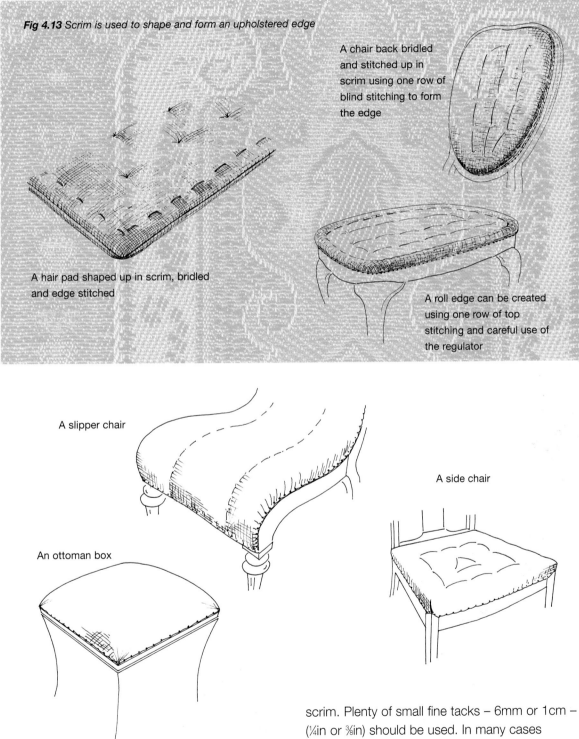

Fig 4.13 *Scrim is used to shape and form an upholstered edge*

A chair back bridled and stitched up in scrim using one row of blind stitching to form the edge

A hair pad shaped up in scrim, bridled and edge stitched

A roll edge can be created using one row of top stitching and careful use of the regulator

A slipper chair

A side chair

An ottoman box

Fig 4.14 *Using 9oz (290g) hessian scrim over first stuffings with 6mm and 1cm (¼in and ⅜in) tacks to make shape on three unsprung items of furniture*

scrim. Plenty of small fine tacks – 6mm or 1cm – (¼in or ⅜in) should be used. In many cases tacking should be as close as 1.3cm (½in). This allows good control of shape and contour and ensures that subsequent stitching is strong.

39

Stuffing ties, arrangement and pattern

As the name implies, stuffing ties are put in to hold and stabilize stuffings and scrim. Once the stitches are in place, edge building can continue. Temporary tacks or skewers can be safely removed, a few at a time, and the tied scrim will remain square and tightly in place. Stuffing ties are formed with a long running stitch, using a two-point needle, and a medium-size twine. The stitch begins and ends on the top surface of the scrim, starting with a slipknot and finishing with half hitches (Fig 4.15). The pattern of the ties should always follow the outline of the piece of work; the spacing of the rows is best kept at about 10cm (4in), or closer on very small pieces of work. After the ties have been stitched in and before tying off, they can be tightened down by working along the ties, lightly compressing the fillings. When an even, flat surface has been created, with stitches all at the same depth, then the last ties can be looped back and tied off with two half hitches. Some examples of stuffing tie patterns are shown in figures 4.16–4.18.

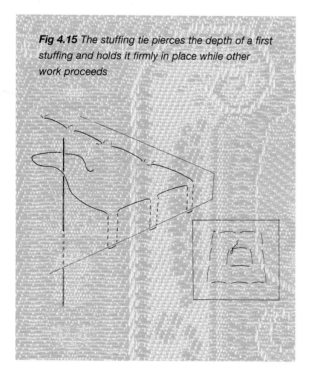

Fig 4.15 *The stuffing tie pierces the depth of a first stuffing and holds it firmly in place while other work proceeds*

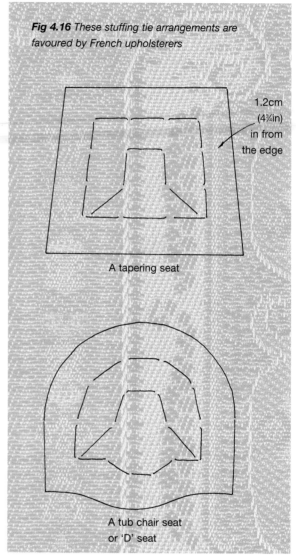

Fig 4.16 *These stuffing tie arrangements are favoured by French upholsterers*

1.2cm (4¾in) in from the edge

A tapering seat

A tub chair seat or 'D' seat

When required, the tightness and depth of stuffing ties can be varied to produce shape, particularly on chair backs and arms. This is a means of creating channels, fluting or pull-ins as a surface design. On unsprung work ties run through the first stuffing to the webbed base, but on sprung areas the stitches stop at the hessian level and should not be taken through the springing, or down to the webbings. If this is done then the ties will simply slacken and will then be ineffective when the springs come to be compressed when the furniture is in use.

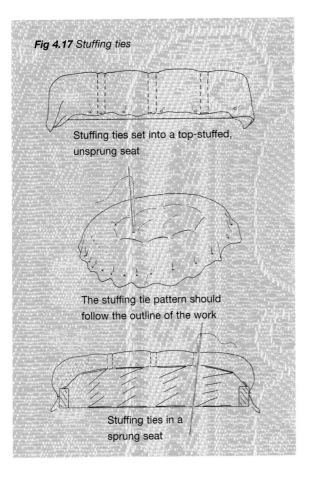

Fig 4.17 *Stuffing ties*

Stuffing ties set into a top-stuffed, unsprung seat

The stuffing tie pattern should follow the outline of the work

Stuffing ties in a sprung seat

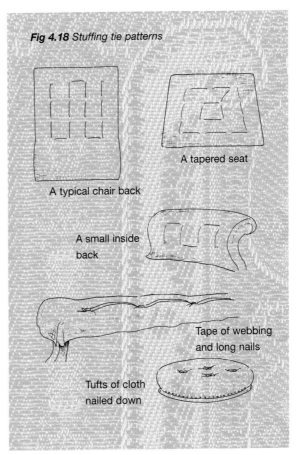

Fig 4.18 *Stuffing tie patterns*

A typical chair back

A tapered seat

A small inside back

Tape of webbing and long nails

Tufts of cloth nailed down

Temporary tacking and skewering

Upholsterers' skewers and long-pins are used in the same way as temporary tacks, to set in place and hold materials (Fig 4.19). There are many occasions when it is necessary to hold linings, scrims and fabrics in place while they are adjusted, checked and matched before permanent fixing. This is good practice and allows for work to be constantly checked before being pulled down permanently. This technique also helps in forming work with a good shape and the aligning of joints, pleats and folds. Use these techniques to set on and adjust fabrics and linings as the upholstery progresses. Tightness, stretch and good line are all essential elements of upholstery, and will help you to produce the sharp, well-manicured finish that you should aim for.

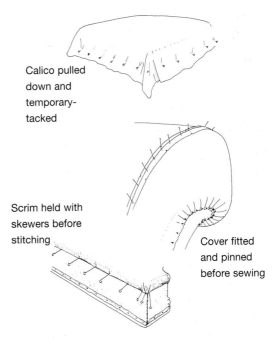

Calico pulled down and temporary-tacked

Scrim held with skewers before stitching

Cover fitted and pinned before sewing

Fig 4.19 *Some examples of temporary fixings*

Making edges and regulating

The regulator has many uses but its main purpose is the moving and regulating of fillings (Fig 4.20). At least two sizes of reg (as it is often referred to) should be kept, a heavy gauge and a medium size, and for very fine regulating through linings and coverings, an old broken smooth point needle or a 4in (10cm) upholstery skewer will do the job well. The regulator is also a very useful holding tool, while scrim or linings are being folded or pleated ready for tacking down.

The regulator is essential when edges are being prepared for stitching. The stitched edge in upholstery and bed-making was first developed in the 18th century. It began as a roll along the edge of a wooden frame, in which a small amount of loose filling was rolled up in linen cloth or scrim, and tacked neatly around French and English chairs. The roll was held down and made firm by a series of simple stitches. This created an edge height above the timber rail and produced upholstery with a flatter surface. Upholstery coverings could then be pulled over or bordered to give a more angular and sharper appearance. The more rows of stitching added to the edge, the firmer and higher the seat above the rail.

From this technique the well seat developed. It has a high edge all around (often referred to as the dead stuffing) creating a well in the centre. The well was then filled to create a comfortable centre area in, for example, a chair seat or chair back. Often the centre was tufted or buttoned as a decoration, as well as to hold the fillings in place.

As an alternative, a firmer more compact seat was developed from this in which the first stuffing was evenly laid all over a seat, covered in scrim and then stitched around the edges. As the edges were tightly turned in and several rows of stitching applied, the scrim became stretched and taut. This is the type of upholstery which we refer to today as 'stitched up' upholstery.

Dug roll or thumb roll edging are very simple versions of edge upholstery. Some variations are shown, right (Fig 4.21). Fillings for the roll can be coir fibre, curled hair, felts or flocks, or any loose filling which will compress into a firm edge roll. Compressed paper is used in the ready-made version which can be bought on the roll or by the metre. Sizes range, from small finger size up to 3.8cm (1½in) diameter.

Stitched-edge upholstery

The well-seat technique is mostly used only as a foundation for buttoning and to create a soft seat or back rest, or as a platform under a cushion. The firmer two-layer method is preferred for most other work. There are two basic stitches used to form an edge of this type; the blind stitch and the top stitch. The blind stitch is made first and

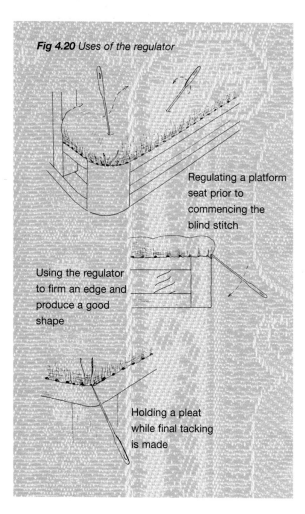

Fig 4.20 Uses of the regulator

Regulating a platform seat prior to commencing the blind stitch

Using the regulator to firm an edge and produce a good shape

Holding a pleat while final tacking is made

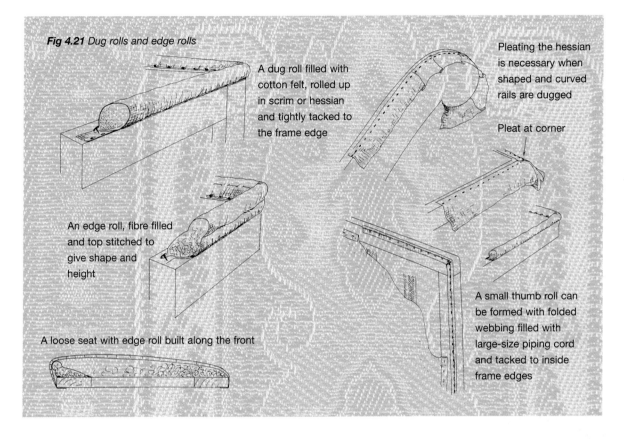

Fig 4.21 *Dug rolls and edge rolls*

A dug roll filled with cotton felt, rolled up in scrim or hessian and tightly tacked to the frame edge

Pleating the hessian is necessary when shaped and curved rails are dugged

Pleat at corner

An edge roll, fibre filled and top stitched to give shape and height

A small thumb roll can be formed with folded webbing filled with large-size piping cord and tacked to inside frame edges

A loose seat with edge roll built along the front

creates a firm foundation for the subsequent rows of top stitching. The blind stitch, so called because it only shows on the face edge of the upholstery and does not pierce the top of the scrim, pulls small amounts of stuffing outwards as the stitch is tightened (Fig 4.22).

Two or more rows of blind stitching can be used, one above the other, when an edge is required to be 3.8cm (1½in) or more, above the rail. Fine flax stitching twine and a two-point needle are used for this type of work. Stitching can begin once the edge has been made, with good amounts of

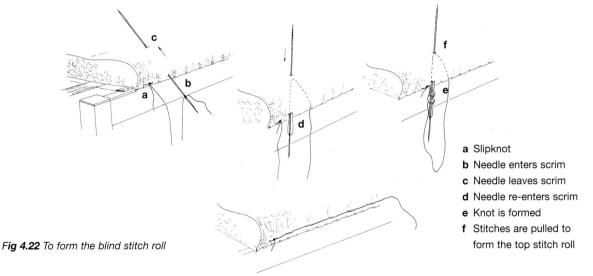

a Slipknot
b Needle enters scrim
c Needle leaves scrim
d Needle re-enters scrim
e Knot is formed
f Stitches are pulled to form the top stitch roll

Fig 4.22 *To form the blind stitch roll*

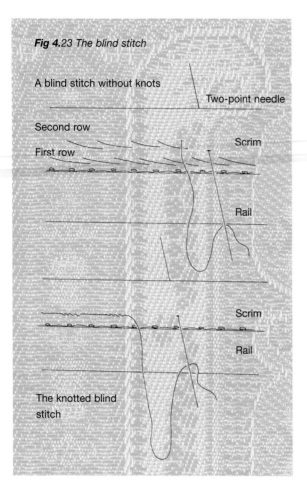

Fig 4.23 *The blind stitch*

A blind stitch without knots

Two-point needle

Second row

First row

Scrim

Rail

Scrim

Rail

The knotted blind stitch

filling, and the scrim turned in and tacked onto the shamfered rail edge. Make the edge firm, well filled and with a small amount of overhang, 6mm (¼in) is an ideal amount.

The stuffing is regulated and the first stitch is put in with a slipknot, the blind stitch is then worked along the edge, beginning with a left-hand end and working to the right (Fig 4.23). A left-handed person may prefer to work in the opposite direction. A good firm pull is required after each stitch, and a leather stitching glove can be used to protect the hand from the sharpness of the twine. When a row of blind stitching is complete the edge can be regulated again to improve its evenness.

Top stitching follows the blind stitching, its function being to pinch and hold the upper part of an edge into a sharp, firm shape (Fig 4.24).

The more rows of top stitching that are applied, usually the sharper the edge becomes. Two rows of top stitching are normal on an average seat edge. A third or fourth row would only be used to gain more height and sharpness.

A top stitch is formed in the same way as a blind stitch, except that the stitches are closer

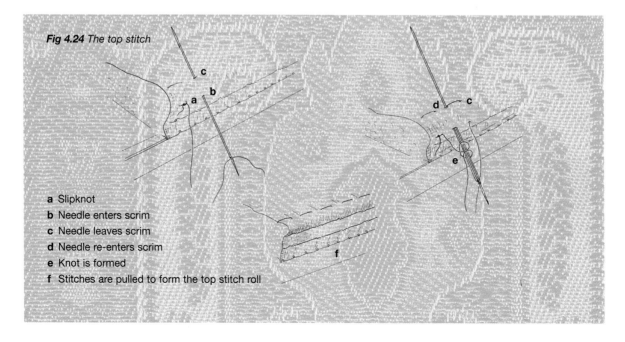

Fig 4.24 *The top stitch*

a Slipknot
b Needle enters scrim
c Needle leaves scrim
d Needle re-enters scrim
e Knot is formed
f Stitches are pulled to form the top stitch roll

together and the twine pierces through the scrim on the top of the edge and shows as an even dotted line of stitches on the surface. As it is tightened the stitch pinches the packed scrim into a neat, sharp edge. The size of the roll is determined by the positioning of the needle and the amount of scrim taken in by the needle. Blind stitches and top stitches can be secured with locking stitch (Fig 4.25).

Edgemaking is an important part of the craft and once learnt is never forgotten. Variations on the basic edge form can then be practised and used when different upholstery styles are needed. For example, diagonal top stitching is a very useful variation and is used a great deal in Europe.

The feather edge is another development, which simply means adding a final top stitch very close to the sharp edge of the scrim. A feather edge can be made with a blanket stitch formation or can be a fine, close version of the top stitch (Fig 4.26). Feather edges are recommended when upholstery is to be bordered, and where a piping or a cord is to be sewn along an edge.

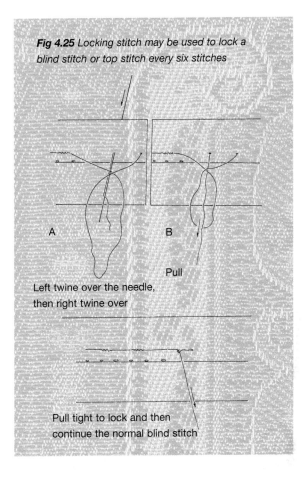

Fig 4.25 Locking stitch may be used to lock a blind stitch or top stitch every six stitches

A　　　　　B

Pull

Left twine over the needle, then right twine over

Pull tight to lock and then continue the normal blind stitch

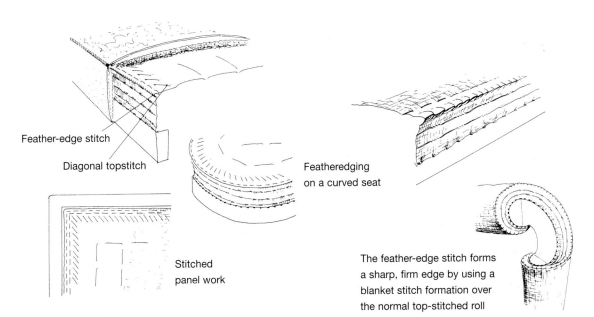

Feather-edge stitch

Diagonal topstitch

Featheredging on a curved seat

Stitched panel work

The feather-edge stitch forms a sharp, firm edge by using a blanket stitch formation over the normal top-stitched roll

Fig 4.26 Feather-edge stitching

Second stuffing, comfort and crown

The second layer of filling in both traditional and modern upholstery, which rests on the foundation stuffing or first stuffing, is designed to provide softness and comfort.

A second stuffing can be one single filling, or, as in many cases a combination of two fillings. For example, a soft foam and some polyester fibre, a rubberized hair and some cotton felt, or loose curled hair and some skin wadding. Choose the filling to suit the type of upholstery that you are doing, and make the depth of the filling adequate, so that a crown is created to give shape and comfort. Very few surfaces on upholstered seating are flat when they are first built and covered. This amount of shape and depth will compensate for the initial wear and tear that a piece of upholstery will get during use.

Depth of filling is an important consideration and the two stuffings can be balanced to give the ideal strength and depth to a piece of work. For example, when a chair back is to be buttoned, the second stuffing into which the buttons will be pulled, needs to be of a good depth. This can be compared with the fillings in a plain unbuttoned seat or back where the two stuffings, first and second, would be about equal in depth. Another good example is the lid on a box ottoman, which needs to have a very high crown if shape, design and proportion are well considered and are in keeping with tradition and good practice. Second stuffings are pulled down tightly to set their shape, before the final covering.

Pulling down in calico

Calico is used in dress making, curtain making, and as a lining material in upholstery. The upholstery term 'pulled down in calico' refers to a piece of upholstery lined and upholstered over the second stuffing, prior to being top covered (Fig 4.27).

It is common practice to line good-quality work with calico. It has many benefits, both to the

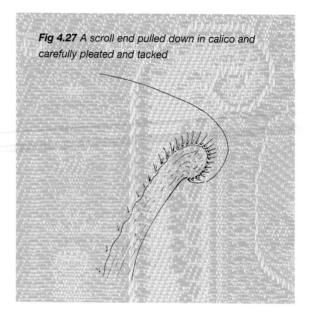

Fig 4.27 *A scroll end pulled down in calico and carefully pleated and tacked*

upholsterer and the user of the upholstery. A calico lining takes the strain and tension before covering is applied. Cuts and shapes can be checked and made more precise. The final covering of an upholstery fabric will give better and longer service when the upholstery is lined.

The flame-proofing of calico to make it fire retardent has become normal practice on certain weights of cloth. This is always specified and labelled. A flame resistant grade can be used wherever the type of furniture being upholstered is covered by the requirements of legislation which requires the upholstery to be fire retardent to a certain standard. For example new furniture produced for sale to the general public, or for use in public buildings may well fall into this category. If you are producing or restoring a piece of work for yourself, then you have the choice as to whether you use fire resistant materials. This is particularly so when a piece of work was designed and made before 1950.

Covering and cutting

The cutting and fitting of covers and linings on chairs, stools and boxes can be one of the most difficult areas of upholstery. All upholsterers will no doubt remember how they have learned by their mistakes or their near misses. In most instances, if a wrong cut is made, there is usually some way of overcoming the problem without having to replace an expensive piece of fabric.

With care and practise, the art of cutting and manipulating fabrics can be learned. It is equally important to learn the reaction of different types of cloth to being cut and stretched. Leather for example, works and cuts very differently from a piece of cotton tapestry, and the difference has to be appreciated. Some fabrics fray very easily, while some will tear with very little resistance. The whole range of upholstery coverings is very wide, but generally it can be said that providing a fabric is recommended for use in upholstery it will be reasonably durable and have good strength.

Most of the cutting required while you are working at the bench, is in the shaping and trimming of covers so that they will fit the frame being upholstered (Fig 4.28). Trimming is also

required at corners and over edges, where pleats and folds are being made (Fig 4.28). Cutting positions have to be determined by assessing depth of filling and positioning cover parts so that the cut being made is in the right place and to the correct depth. Most cover parts can be partly cut and partly tucked away before a cut is fully made. This method is by far the safest as well as being the most accurate.

By temporarily tacking the piece in place, and using the fingers to tuck the fabric partly away, the depth and position can easily be found. Careful snipping of the covering will allow it to be pushed into place as a test for accuracy. Further snipping may then be necessary to complete good fit.

The method and results of cutting are often closely related to the way in which a piece of cover is first fixed and positioned. Positioning is all-important and must be reasonably good before any attempt to cut is made. Use the thread lines in a fabric as your guide to accurate cutting.

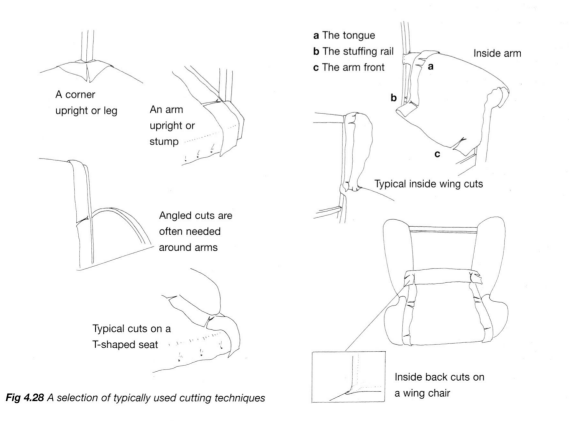

A corner upright or leg

An arm upright or stump

Angled cuts are often needed around arms

Typical cuts on a T-shaped seat

a The tongue
b The stuffing rail
c The arm front

Inside arm

Typical inside wing cuts

Inside back cuts on a wing chair

Fig 4.28 *A selection of typically used cutting techniques*

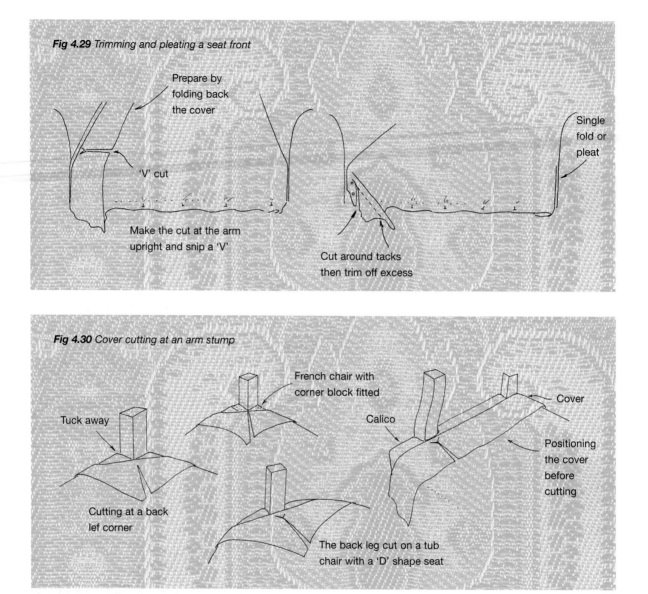

Fig 4.29 *Trimming and pleating a seat front*

Prepare by folding back the cover

'V' cut

Make the cut at the arm upright and snip a 'V'

Cut around tacks then trim off excess

Single fold or pleat

Fig 4.30 *Cover cutting at an arm stump*

Tuck away

French chair with corner block fitted

Calico

Cover

Positioning the cover before cutting

Cutting at a back lef corner

The back leg cut on a tub chair with a 'D' shape seat

Pleating and folding

It is mostly at the corners of a seat or a chairback that the pleating and folding of fabrics will occur. This is necessary in order to remove surplus fabric and allow the corner to be finished and pulled down tightly and to be neatened.

A well-pulled and tightly formed corner is often the secret of good upholstery which looks clean and well tailored. There are one or two basic rules to follow but as always, you can develop your own ideas and interpret a corner shape to suit the piece and its style. The general rule is for a square corner to have a single fold or pleat and for a rounded corner to have two inverted folds or pleats in a 'V' formation (Fig 4.29).

Another example is the corner with a long curve or the completely circular seat both of which will require multiple pleating to even out the fullness of the fabric. As long as the pleats are tight and sharp this treatment will be acceptable and pleasing to the eye (Fig 4.30).

Victorian s
edge is ma
stitch is sp
knots and
squeeze th
edge (Fig 4
sailing, wh
used to ma

Fig 4.37

The back
One of the
normally wo
as a substit
continuous
sewn seam
trimmings s
stitch would
the surface
(1.3cm) (Fig

Fig 4.36

Order of working

Each upholstery project that is undertaken has to be dealt with according to its design, shape and function. In chair work the sequence in which the upholstery is built onto the frame is a very set process. It applies to most conventionally shaped chairs and sofas. The more recent the piece, then the more likely there may be a change in the method of working. The average armchair or wing-chair should be dealt with by completing the insides first, then the outsides (Fig 4.31).

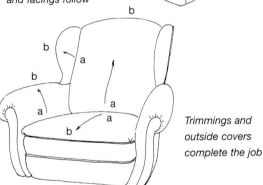

Fig 4.31 Inside coverings commence with inside arms, inside wings, followed by inside back and then the seat

*First fixings at **a**, then pulled and fixed at **b**, borders and facings follow*

Trimmings and outside covers complete the job

1 Upholster and cover the inside of the arms and wings.
2 Put in the inside back and its covering.
3 Build and upholster the seat.
4 Apply trimmings, such as pipings, cords or ruche, to the edges if desired.
5 Line, pad and cover the outside wings and then arms.
6 Line, pad and cover the outside back.
7 The outsides complete, turn the chair over and fix the bottom edges all round.
8 Add a bottom covering of hessian or black cloth.

This method of working is practised by most upholsterers and will be second nature to them. It allows you to work easily and freely without being obstructed at tuckaways, and makes for easier and more accurate cutting.

There is, of course, always the exception. It may sometimes be necessary to upholster a job completely in calico using the normal methods and then to cover the chair in its top cover, repeating the same basic sequence again. This would be normal practice when a chair is not being completely stripped, but just recovered with a new top stuffing added to replace the old.

Loose cushions in seats and backs are usually measured for, cut and made up as soon as the inside covering is completed. This allows for adjustments to be made where necessary, before outsides are fixed.

French armchairs are another exception and are very often dealt with by putting the seat in first, and then continuing with the remainder, as above. This is because French chairs do not have tacking rails or stuffing rails, two names for the same thing, that is, the narrow timber rails set around the inside of the seat about 3in (75mm) above the main seat rails. These are common in English chairs, but in French chair-making steel wires are put in by the upholsterer in order to create the tuckaway.

Hand sewing

A lock stitch

The lock stitch seam is made with a circular needle and some strong linen twine and is used to sew hessian, scrim and lining materials together (Fig 4.32). Making these joins is part of the upholstery process at the bench. The two pieces to be joined are trimmed and turned in, and then skewered to hold them in place. Stitches are simply formed by catching each ply, drawing them together and locking with a single knot about every ½in (1.3cm).

Runni

A runn

holding

perma

4.33).

out of

or lock

the se:

pre-se

sewn,

for exa

bolster

Slip st

This is

that inv

great d

locating

4.34). l

Piped or welted seams are extremely strong and tend to make attractive joints on any furnishing fabric, and are therefore used a great deal. Reinforced seams may be used for their strengthening function, or applied simply to enhance an edge or joint.

The plain seam, used with the appropriate needle and thread, for example, a size 18 or 19 needle and a size 40 or 36 thread is a good choice for virtually all upholstery sewing. Set the sewing machine stitch length to ten stitches to the inch for fabrics and eight stitches to the inch for leather. Only when very thin fine fabrics are being sewn should there be a need to reduce the stitch length and the needle and thread size. A very large stitch length can occasionally be used when a top stitch is sewn in for decorative reasons, for example in leather work.

Hand springing

Upholstery springs of the traditional type are double cone springs, sometimes referred to as waisted or hourglass. The modern alternatives are tension springs, either close coiled or sinuous, often referred to as zig-zag. They are all manufactured from spring steel wires which vary in thickness depending on the hardness required.

Choosing springs

Spring wire thicknesses are measured and specified in swg (standard wire gauge). A table is shown on page 16 of those gauges most used and their particular applications. An example would be 10swg, which is a good choice for the seat of a small armchair. The height of the spring also needs to be chosen, depending on the chair and its rail height above the webbing. Stand a tape measure on the webbing and measure vertically to at least 2in (5cm) above the rail edge. This height will ensure that the springs will work and compress during use without the springs or their lashing being too strained.

Nine 6in (15cm) springs is a typical treatment for a seat of average proportions. Another row of three can be added when a similar seat is a little deeper or wider (Fig 4.38).

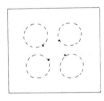

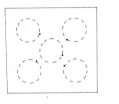

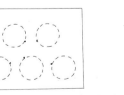

Numbers of springs will range from four to sixteen in seats with less needed in backs. Spring knots should be kept in the diagonal, with outer edges always clear

An extra row of three may often be placed over the stretcher rail for the longer seat. Two extra springs are added for a *chaise-longue* end

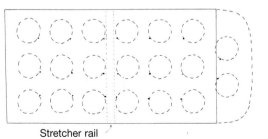

Spring layout for a large chair seat

Stretcher rail

Fig 4.38 *Typical spring arrangements*

Lashing springs

Plain lashing is produced with two lines of cord, one running front to back and the second running from side to side. A further two rows of lashing can be added diagonally to form a method often referred to as star lashing. Plain lashing and star lashing are applied over the surface of the springs and link the tops of all the springs in two or three directions.

Another method is centre lashing which may be used as an addition to the other two or may be used as an alternative. When used as an alternative the feel of the seat will be softer, because the top half of the springs is free, and they are held in place at their centres. In a well-lashed seat the outer springs should be slightly tilted towards the edges of the frame, and the centre springs should remain upright (Fig 4.39).

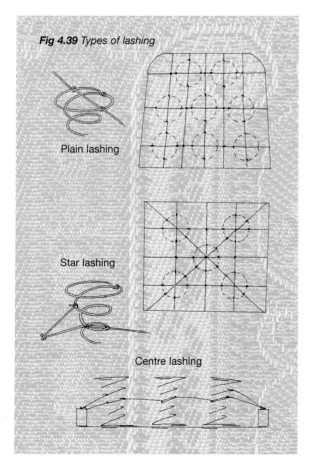

Fig 4.39 Types of lashing

Plain lashing

Star lashing

Centre lashing

Finishing off

Both modern and traditional methods of closing and finishing can be used on chairs and settees of any age. However, the slip stitch is still the most versatile and the most widely used, particularly when small projects are being reupholstered and recovered. Modern techniques such as back-tacking, tack-trim, and Y-strip, depend much on good timber rails being the right shape and in the right place. Slip stitching of outside arms, outside backs and facings allows the upholsterer the freedom to stitch and finish the work wherever it is easiest, and where the cover will turn and hug the frame shape best. Whenever possible the outside areas should be well lined and padded. This is always good practice and helps to give a well upholstered appearance. Both skin wadding, polyester wadding and cotton felts should be used generously before closing and final covering.

The use of bottom and under-seat linings will vary according to the type of work being dealt with (Fig 4.40). Very often early and antique unsprung work was not underlined. Where frames have become particularly rough, or badly treated in the past, it may be best to line and cover up the undersides. Generally webbed and sprung upholstery, which is upholstered in the traditional way, is finished and lined with hessian or black cotton lining cloth, hessian being the more traditional, as a dust cover under a seat.

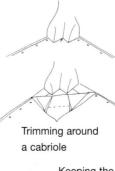

Trimming around a cabriole

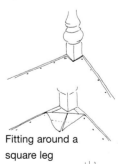

Fitting around a square leg

Keeping the bottom open by fitting a lining before webbing

Fig 4.40 Fitting bottom linings

5 Identifying upholstered furniture

This chapter will take a close look at the different parts of various pieces of upholstered furniture, mostly from a historic view. A broad knowledge of the materials, fabrics and upholstery methods used by upholsterers and designers in the past can help us to date and value a piece that we may be considering buying or restoring. Recognizing a piece of work and being able to identify origin will also help with the decisions that have to be made regarding possible refurbishment and treatments.

If you are able to identify and appreciate the differences between products made in Europe and America, you will find the process of buying and working on upholstered seating is made even more interesting.

Castors and domes

On chairs settees and stools the all-brass castor with a brass wheel will generally indicate that the design of the piece will have been early Victorian, William IV or possibly Regency. Look for the brass wheel, which is quite slim and about 1in to 1¼in (2.5cm to 3cm) diameter, it will often indicate that the work is fairly early 19th century.

Brass castors with china wheels, brown, black or white will generally indicate that a piece of seating was made from the middle of the 19th century and possibly into the Edwardian period, around 1910. From that time the castor became less popular and gradually began to disappear from use. The simple metal glide or 'dome of silence' was gradually to take over and be in use for the next 30 years or so.

Legs and feet

The design of the chair leg or the foot, will tell us a great deal about a piece of seating. The material from which it is made, its shape and design and often its proportions will help us to recognize a genuine article and to be able to date and value a piece of upholstered furniture. Immediately a chair, for example, is recognized as being made during

a particular period, because of a leg or a foot style, it can then be researched and compared with similar pieces, from records that you may have or from books or archive material. This recognition and information is then a useful confirmation of the work and its precise design.

The reconstruction of the upholstery, its detail, the decorative trimmings, and so on can then be decided on and either imitated exactly or kept in proportion and arrangement with the original. For recognition purposes, leg design is an important feature of anything that is upholstered, particularly with stuff-over and fully upholstered work. This is because timber show-wood parts are permanent and mostly will be original. The upholstered parts of a chair, for example, may well have been replaced or changed during the life of the piece.

Fabrics and covers

When the upholstery is being removed in preparation for restoration or recovering of a chair, then the covering fabric is the first and most obvious identifying material. Depending on the age of a piece, the cover may be original or there may be, as is often the case, more than one layer of cover evident. It is not unusual to find as many as four different covers on a sofa or chair that may be a hundred years old or more. Quite often fabrics are replaced or simply covered over with more fabric to give a fresh look and to bring a chair in line with current fashion.

Show-wood

Many pieces of upholstered furniture have plenty of polished wood or show-wood areas. This helps us a great deal to identify and confirm a particular style. A good example is the furniture made in the second half of the 19th century, when walnut was the most commonly used timber in all kinds of domestic furniture.

Prior to this, a very attractive timber called rosewood was widely used and became very fashionable for a time, and before that, in the second half of the 18th century, good quality mahogany was typical of the Georgian period, a very widely used stable and attractive wood. Equally, the surface finish used on a show-wood timber will have been a French polish applied by hand, and finally finished with a natural wax.

Post-1950 however, the surface finish on show-wood areas is more likely to have been lacquered, using spray finishing techniques and a nitro cellulose film. Another interesting development is the fashion for japanned and painted surfaces, which occurred during the mid- to late-Victorian era. Surfaces were mainly black with some inlaid and some painted features. Very much the height of fashion at the time.

It was during the late 19th century and early 20th century that oak became the chosen timber for a style of furniture designed and made during the Arts and Crafts period. Oak as a furniture-making timber remained very popular well into the 20th century.

During the period between world wars I and II it is interesting to note that the popularity of walnut increased once again. Walnut reappeared not as a solid timber, as before, but as a veneer applied on to the new plywoods being produced at the time. The reason for this may have been a scarcity of good hardwoods, as well as the need to produce and reproduce furniture at a higher rate and at a generally lower cost. It is often the case that world events and the resulting social climates influence the way in which we use our natural resources.

Webbings

Upholstery webbings are the foundation of most types of handmade fabric-covered seating. They have quite a history in themselves and can tell us something about the origin and the age of a piece of upholstery. In traditional work, webbings basically have not changed very much over the last 300 years or so. Turn a chair upside down or remove the underside dust cover, and the webbings will be visible. Immediately it may be possible to determine if a chair or a stool, for example, is British, European or American. Each of these tends to have it's own characteristic webbing types.

Getting to know and recognize these variations in webbing size, colour and weave is both interesting and of great help when you are searching for evidence of origin, either simply as a point of interest or as a 'need to know' requirement in order to ensure that the choice of replacement will be sympathetic.

Webbings made and used in mainland Europe will be the wide type and will be around 9cm (3½in) wide, colours will vary but are mostly brown with colour lines running along their length. The webbing arrangement will be close with each web almost touching it's neighbour. Even if the webbings are missing and have already been removed, the tack holes will tell you how the webs were originally arranged.

In comparison, the webbings on a British-made chair are relatively narrow with an average width of 5cm (2in). The fixing arrangement will also be quite

Fig 5.0 *Some examples of old webbings taken from antique chairs*

different, in that the webbings will be well spaced, with at least an 2.5cm (1in) between the fixings.

Another interesting comparison is the difference in weave structure between English webbings and those used by American and European upholsterers. Best English types are twill woven in a herringbone pattern and will be black and white or brown and white in colour. The wider American and French webbings, for example, will be generally plain woven and made from a slightly thicker yarn.

There are many other features which will tell us about the origins of webbings and the pieces of furniture in which they have been used. Age is just one example. The history and development of the upholstery webbing can be quite fascinating and can be very useful as a tool for measuring the history of a chair.

Springs and springing

Springs in upholstered seating, particularly on seating made in the 19th century influenced the size and the general design of all kinds of chairs, sofas and ottomans. We can learn a lot from the type of spring that has been used in a piece of upholstery. Springs for use in furniture were first patented in the 1830s but they were not used in great quantities until later in the Victorian era. Early springs (dating from around 1850) were quite heavy and crudely made, and their ends were bound with fine wire. Later examples had a metal clip at each end of the spring, which was mechanically clamped on to the wire ends. Then from around 1890 springs for upholstery were machine made, they had a lighter gauge of wire and a single knot or turn to finish them. Such springs were in turn superseded in around 1930 by the new versions made from spring steel with a double knot machine-twisted to finish them. The excellent performance of spring steel meant that wire thicknesses could be reduced and the number of coils in a spring reduced, all much more lightweight than before.

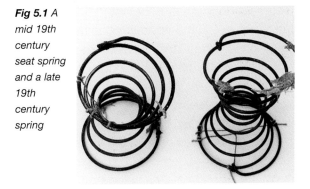

Fig 5.1 A mid 19th century seat spring and a late 19th century spring

A great deal of the furniture that was refurbished and restored during the late 19th and early 20th centuries was sprung, in an attempt to make earlier work more comfortable, and hence more in line with the current fashion for sprung upholstery. It was not until the middle of the 20th century that another dramatic change in seating suspension, took place. The compression spring was largely replaced by the tension spring system which was much more adaptable, lightweight and less costly to apply. These new methods were basically lateral systems, and allowed a good degree of comfort without the bulk and depth of the older compression springs.

This history of the developments in springing can be used to identify and date chairs and settees with a good deal of accuracy. Before restoration begins, questions can be asked as we look for evidence of early and original upholstery work. Ask questions about the present condition, should it be sprung? Was it originally sprung? Do we really need to put springs back into a chair when it may be quite delicate structurally or the design would be much better suited to a simple top-stuffed unsprung treatment?

Fillings

Prior to 1952 in the United Kingdom, when the Rag Flock Act was passed, which aimed to make upholstery and bedding a cleaner and more healthy product, fillings for upholstery could be made and processed from almost anything.

Hence the huge variety of natural filling materials that were used in the industry and can now be found in the furniture that we restore and reupholster today. Seaweed, wood wool, animal hair, flocks, grasses, wool fleece, feathers and down are but a few of the fillings likely to be evident in old upholstery and bedding.

Many of these came into use during particular periods of furniture design and represent the development of upholstery. In the long list of fillings, those of animal origin are almost certainly the ones which go back in history the furthest, and it is interesting that they have stood the test of time, and are still in use today. Bi-products of the meat industry are being used and processed in a variety of different forms.

Most of the other fillings that are generally vegetable-based have come in and out of popularity. Cotton is perhaps the one vegetable fibre filling that has outlasted its competitors and also remains a very useful favourite in today's upholstery, both traditional and modern. The prefabrication of fillings was another significant development and happened on a large scale during the years 1930–50. Prior to this, upholstery fillings were loose fibrous materials and had to be handled and layered in place by the upholsterer, a very labour intensive business.

Curled horse hair, pig and cow hair are without doubt the best of the traditional fillings, and will be found in good-quality work from the early 18th century until the middle of the 20th century. Grasses and flax fibres also have a long history, particularly in mainland Europe, and were all used as basic foundation stuffings. The range of softer fillings such as feathers, down and cotton wadding will also be found in good quality chairs and furnishings, for example top stuffings and cushion fillings.

It was during and after World War II that upholstery foams were developed, and first used in sheet and moulded forms. Early plastic foams such as those made from polyether and polyester became generally available and used post-1960 and these were soon superseded by the new generation of high resilience, urethane foams. Except for curled hair animal fillings, most of the other varieties are replaced when a piece of upholstery is restored and rebuilt.

Stitched-edge work

Discovering good stitched-edge upholstery work in an old chair is always fascinating and will help us to discern the history of a chair or sofa. Because stitched-edge work is a very individual skill, it would be unusual to find completely identical pieces. Stitched edges are hand-crafted so each one will be worked slightly differently. Looking closely at a piece of good edge stitching is rather like reading a person's handwriting; the words will have the same meaning whoever they are written by but their character will be individual. Blind stitching, top stitching and feather edge stitching are all combined and used to produce a firm supporting edge line in traditional upholstery work.

In the United Kingdom blind stitching and top stitching are usually knotted to hold each stitch tightly as the work progresses. Locking the stitch will usually occur approximately every sixth stitch. In France, however, the upholsterer seldom knots the individual stitches, because the work is done using a slightly different technique and a large curved needle, and not a straight one as in English work. The differences can be spotted quite easily and will usually tell us where a piece has originated. Only the final top-stitch row is knotted in French examples, and also the corner stitching is much more complex than the English equivalents.

Inner fabrics and linings

When the inner linings and supporting cloths in an old chair are made from linen, then a piece is likely to be early Victorian or prior to this. Linen is reasonably easy to identify; it is finer and has a softer feel than the jute materials, such as hessians, which superceded it. Linens will turn a pale grey colour with age and are likely to be found as base cloths, immediately over webbings, and as lightweight scrims immediately over first stuffings. Although, softer and cooler to the touch, linen cloths are equally as strong and robust as jute materials which are found in later examples.

Tarpaulins, hessians and scrims, all made from jute fibre, gradually took over from linens during the late 19th century. These generally become a dark ginger brown colour with age, and will also tend to be brittle after exposure to light or to damp conditions, over a number of years.

Calico linings

Cotton calico has changed very little over the 19th and 20th centuries and is still manufactured and used as the first covering in good-quality upholstery. Early calico tended to be very fine and lightweight but none-the-less very suitable as a first covering before the covering fabric. Calico of any reasonable age will almost certainly have changed in colour from white to a dull grey. This will be caused by soiling and light penetration.

Decoration and trimmings

Style and fashion in furnishing has always influenced the way in which upholstered furniture has been decorated and finished. In the past some period styles and their associated upholstery have shown very little desire for the decorative. The Regency period for example, and the much later Arts and Crafts movement in design, opted for the more plain and austere outlines. Whereas, in complete contrast, the long Victorian period showed a distinct demand for a very decorative and fussy style in decoration.

However, each period has its own particular attractions and we can use these differences to help identify pieces of furniture, and then, if we wish, we can use our traditional materials and techniques to reproduce or to change a look or a style.

Removing the old covering and the basic upholstery materials from a chair will very often allow you to discover its history as you work through the layers inside. A chair back or the surface of a stool, may well have been tufted or buttoned when it was first made, but subsequent upholstery coverings have disguised the original effect. We then have the choice of reworking the current but worn-out incarnation of the upholstery or using new materials to rebuild the earlier design.

Trimmings

Trimmings such as cording, gimps, braids and fringes are all available today in a great variety of colourways and styles. Choose those that go well with your fabrics and at the same time suit the style of the piece. Use the evidence that you find to help you choose your replacements.

As an example, a continuous row of tiny holes along the bottom edge of a chair seat will usually mean that the work was originally finished with brass nailing. Chairs and settees of the late 18th century in both France and England were very often finished and decorated with close nailing in brass or antique on brass. French versions often had a gimp or a braid running under the nailing.

Spaced nailing, where the brass nails are set about an inch apart, with or without a banding, was a technique used very early in the 18th century. This style of finish became very popular again in the early 20th century. Fabric-covered studs or nails will also be found on chairs in the Edwardian period.

Fig 5.2 *Fringe, nails, cords, gimps and tassel*

6 Upholstery styles and designs

The design of a piece of upholstery and the way in which it is built is an important part of understanding how a chair works to provide comfort. There are lots of different variations, but most of these are based on traditional, tried-and-tested methods. The upholstery design and its depth, proportion and shape is an integral part of a whole chair or settee. For example, some seats have a loose cushion that provides depth and comfort, whereas others do not need a cushion, but are built using fixed upholstery. Another interesting comparison is the difference between a sprung and an unsprung upholstered seat, with the sprung version generally appearing larger and deeper than the other. This chapter outlines some of the variations and principal upholstery methods from which you can select a suitable treatment. These variations are also very often related to the surface treatment or covering. When a chair back, for example, is to be deep buttoned, then a 'well' needs to be created, so that there will be a good depth of stuffing ready for the buttoning.

These examples illustrate the importance of planning ahead so that as the upholstery is being built the end result can be kept clearly in mind.

Loose seat or drop-in seat

This is a basic hardwood frame which can be easily removed from a chair for upholstery. The frame has shaped and chamfered edges and, once upholstered, is located inside a chair seat or back by sitting it in a rebate or using dowel pegs. Loose seat frames are also screwed in place through corner blocks.

An alternative type of loose seat is the plywood seat frame which is simply a strong plywood shape about 1cm (⅜in) thick, cut to fit on to a chair seat or back after it has been upholstered. Each method uses the materials in a different way. Over time, they have been developed to suit seating styles of different periods.

- Queen Anne
- Regency
- French traditional
- English modern

Fig 6.0 *Loose seat upholstery in a Queen Anne chair*

Projects and Gallery

7 Projects

8 Gallery

7 Projects

The projects here are presented in order of difficulty so that an increasing level of skill is gradually acquired. Depending on your requirements you will be able to select those that you find most interesting or most challenging. Alternatively, follow and work through the eleven projects as closely as possible.

The work illustrated represents a wide range of basic techniques, from simple webbed foundations to some quite challenging shaped, stitched-edge seating, where there are very few straight lines. In complete contrast there are two pieces that use very modern materials and techniques, and these introduce the beginner to foams, glues and synthetic waddings.

Emphasis is placed on the development of hand skills and the way in which shapes are built and produced in attractive and comfortable upholstery.

Project 1
A mahogany stool with drop-in seat

loose or drop-in seat frame in a stool or dining chair is a very common form of conventional upholstered seating. It makes an excellent small upholstery project for the beginner to try out. A seat of this kind can be given the modern or the traditional treatment, depending on your preference and the age of the piece of furniture.

Materials used

- Brown and white English webbing
- 14oz (390g) jute tarpaulin
- Linen mattress twine
- Curled hair, about 0.75 lb (0.4 kg)
- New cotton felt
- Cotton calico (loomstate)
- Cotton skin wadding
- ½in and ⅜in (1.3cm and 1cm) fine tacks
- Black bottom lining
- Cotton/viscose print 39in (1m)

Method

1 The stool for this project was chosen for its attractive style that is based on an early 18th-century design. The stool frame has been carefully restored. The original beech loose-seat frame has been lost and so a new one was made, and carefully fitted to sit into the rebated edge of the main frame. A space of about ⅛in (3mm) all around the frame edge has been allowed for the eventual thickness of the calico and the upholstery fabric covering.

2 In preparation for the upholstery the sharp inner edges of the seat frame are removed with a rasp.

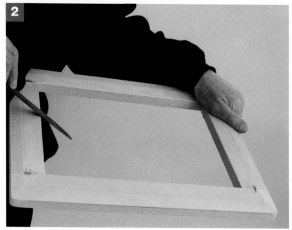

70

3 Using English brown and white webbing the seat is webbed with a four and two arrangement that is tacked along the centres of the beech rails. To avoid the webbing curling when strained, the ½in (13mm) fine tacks are set close to the web edges.

4 The upholstery continues with a covering of 14oz (390g) tarpaulin, tacked with ⅜in (1cm) fine tacks and pulled hand tight, before trimming and turning. To get a good tight base with the tarpaulin, the long side is tacked first and then pulled by hand to its opposite side.

5 Now the stuffing ties, which are called bridle ties, are put in to hold and control the first stuffing. The back-stitch formation used here catches about an inch (2.5cm) of the tarpaulin, but not the webbings.

6 Our first stuffing is loose curled hair, which is an 80/20 mixture of pig and cow hair. Work the hair under the ties, evenly over the seat, to a thickness of about 1½in (4cm). Usually two small handfuls are pushed under each loop to give a good density. The second stuffing is applied directly over the hair filling and is a thick white cotton felt. If this is not available, a wool felt will do the job equally well. Trim the felt with the fingers to feather it off at the edges, leaving enough to cover all the hair filling.

7 Measure for and cut the calico with a good allowance for working and pulling. About 73–4in (7.5cm–10cm) is normally enough. The calico is set on and temporary tacked, with two tacks at the centre of each side.

8 Work out from each centre fixing towards the corners, adding more tacks as the cloth is stretched over and at the same time along the edges towards the corners. Ensure that no filling creeps over the edge and that the face edge is flat. When all four sides are temporary tacked, the corners can be adjusted, pulled very tightly and one tack driven in permanently at the centre of each corner. Check each side for evenness at the edges and add more temporary tacks as necessary. A small square of the calico is then cut from each corner to reduce the bulk of the folded cloth.

9 Turn in, fold and pleat the excess calico at either side of the corners. The pleats should be tight and as small as possible.

10 When the corners are well pulled and the calico evenly set over the edge, the resulting pleats will be small and equal in length.

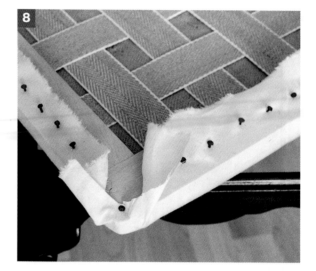

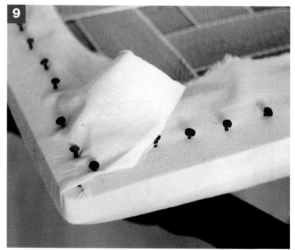

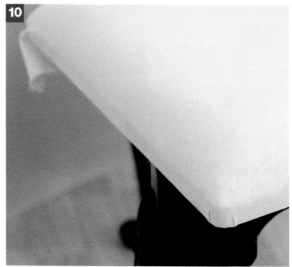

11 This picture shows clearly how flat and clear the edges are of stuffing so that the seat will fit neatly into the stool. A piece of skin wadding is cut and trimmed to fit the seat as the covering fabric is applied.

12 Set the cover on by fixing with temporary tacks at the centres of each long side. The cover is carefully centred and marked with chalk or a notch, which then matches with a centre mark on the seat. This is particularly important when the cover has a pattern. The fabric is well tensioned in all directions and fixed with temporary tacks before the corners are dealt with in the same way as the calico.

13 To reduce bulk at the corners, trim away as much fabric as possible, before folding, pleating and permanently tacking down.

14 The seat is completed with a black cotton lining cloth, turned in and tacked to cover all the earlier fixings. The drop-in seat is pushed well down into the stool's rebated frame.

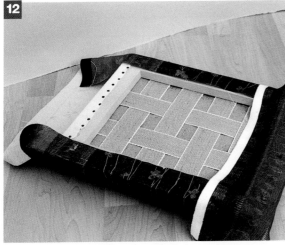

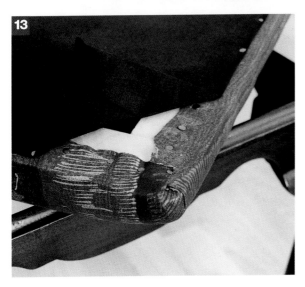

A small Edwardian country-style armchair

This upholstery project has a pinstuffed seat (sometimes referred to as a pincushion seat) that is upholstered into rebated seat rails. The upholstery is slim and quite delicate compared with stuff-over examples, and care has to be taken to protect the show-wood surrounds. About half the seat-rail width has been allowed for the upholstery, the remainder is polished and waxed. This chair design is very typical of many pieces made during the early part of the 20th century.

Materials used

- Black and white English webbing
- 14oz (390gm) hessian
- Mattress twine
- Curled hair mixture, about 0.7 lb (0.9kg)
- Cotton skin wadding
- Calico
- Striped cotton/rayon velour 39in (1 metre)
- Oxford gimp 79in (2 metres)

Method

1 Our project begins at the rebuilding stage. Many of the large tack holes, left by previous upholstery, have been carefully filled and smoothed over by sanding. A mixture of wood glue and fine sawdust has been used as a filler, and some of the larger holes have been filled by pushing a cocktail stick that has been dipped in glue deeply into each. The sticks are trimmed off level after the glue has set, usually about five hours later. Preparation of this kind is occasionally necessary in order to consolidate tacking surfaces, before any new upholstery is applied. When timber rails become very peppered with tack holes from repeated upholstery work, we have to make decisions about condition, and try to ensure that our intended new work does not add more damage to an already very dry and delicate framework.

2 The seat frame is webbed with three webs each way, interwoven and tacked using 1.3cm (½in) fine tacks, along the centre of the rebate space. 1.3cm (½in) staples would also be very acceptable as a fixing in these conditions.

3 Take care when using the web stretcher directly on polished surfaces. A piece of leather can be fixed permanently to the end of the tool or some form of protective padding used when needed.

4 The addition of a black cotton lining cloth on small chairs, put in before the webbings, is an option that can always be considered. It provides a neat dust cover for the underside of a seat, and can be inserted into any small top-stuffed piece of upholstery.

5 A good 366g or 390g (12oz or 14oz) hessian is tacked and strained, hand tight, over the webbings using ⅜in (1cm) fine tacks. This produces a firm tight surface onto which the filling can be tied.

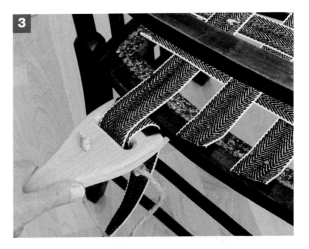

6 Using a mattress twine and a 15cm (6in) curved needle the bridle ties are sewn in, each stitch about the width of the hand in a back stitch formation.

7 As filling progresses over the seat, tease the hair with the fingers to open it up and blend the hair filling into an even layer, with no lumps or hollow spots.

8 The hair filling has to be well insulated by using a layer of cotton skin wadding, both under and over the calico covering. The calico is set onto the seat, four square, using temporary tacks at all four sides, and pulled to a good tightness.

9 The calico is then stretched out tightly towards the corners and fixed. No filling is allowed to creep under or interfere with the tacking.

Beginning at the back of the seat, ease the calico down and add tacks about 1in (2.5cm) apart. Stroke the calico surface towards the front and fix again. The seat sides are then dealt with in the same way.

10 Finally, stretch the calico hard into each corner rebate and tack down.

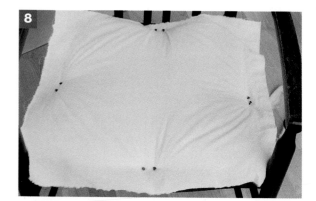

Check the edges for evenness as the tacks are hammered permanently home. If preferred, all the fixings for the calico in a seat of this kind can be made with ⅜in (1cm) gimp pins, which are generally finer and have small heads. Another layer of skin wadding is cut and carefully fitted to the outline of the seat then trimmed a few millimetres short of the tacking line.

11 Using gimp pins, to a matching colour if possible, set the upholstery fabric onto the seat along the back edge. At this point the fabric is centred to ensure that any stripes or patterns are lined up with the centre of the chair seat. A tape measure can be used if necessary. The cover is eased, tightened and fixed using the sequence that was used for the calico. Lift gimp pins where necessary and adjust the tension of the fabric to create an even edge fixing, before hammering them home permanently. Trim the upholstery fabric close to the tacking line to ensure a finish which is in line and parallel with the chair-seat rail edges.

12 An Oxford gimp was chosen for the seat finish. This was glued down with a clear fabric adhesive and the gimp was carefully mitred at each corner. The starting point for a braid or gimp finish is usually just inside one of the back corners.

13 The completed seat.

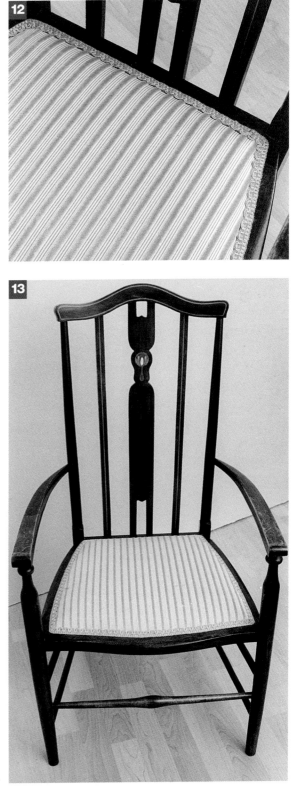

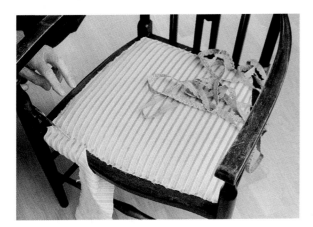

Project 3
Pouffe, an occasional seat or foot stool

Materials used

- Reconstituted chip foam (6lb (2.7kg) density)
- Polyurethane seat foam (35 grade)
- Polyester wadding (4oz (110g) weight)
- Spray adhesive
- Upholstery twine
- Machine thread (36 corespun)
- Black cotton lining
- Knitted pile fabric 39in (1 metre)

Method

1 The design for this project is a simple circular floor seat made from a polyurethane upholstery foam called chip foam or reconstituted foam. It is the heaviest of the foam grades used for upholstery and is very dense, with good weight and support properties. Because the pouffe has no inner hard framework, it is soft and informal and so is ideal for use in a child's room or a playroom and as an occasional piece of seating.

2 The foam interior has been cut from a large block and measures 16in in diameter by 10in high (40cm by 25cm). A suitable interior can also be built from sheet chipfoam by cutting a number of circles and gluing them together. The top layer of 1in (2.5cm) is cut from a normal seat-grade foam.

3 The foam is measured from its top outer edge down to the centre of the base, about 16½in (41cm), and this was recorded for use when cutting the covering fabric.

4 The foam is used as a template to mark out the upholstery fabric, and a sewing allowance of ½in (1.5cm) is added. A metre of thick-pile upholstery fabric, which is fairly robust and can withstand the type of use that pouffes and foot stools tend to get, is used for the covering. A soft white chalk is used to mark out the cover parts. If preferred, a paper or card template can be cut and used for the marking out.

5 A fabric width of 59in (130cm) is perfect for a small pouffe of this size, and allows plenty of excess over the length required for the border, or

side wall. The measurement taken earlier is used to cut the border height and is drawn on to the fabric across the whole width and then cut. The length of the border is trimmed at the sewing stage.

6 A piece of black cotton lining is cut and glued with a spray adhesive onto the base of the foam. This provides a bottom lining and a finish to the base, and hides the foam interior.

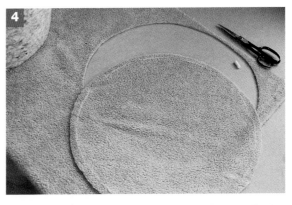

7 4oz (110gm) of polyester wadding is cut and fitted to cover the foam top and the foam walls. The wadding is held in place with a foam spray adhesive, lightly sprayed on both surfaces.

8 With the circular piece of top fabric laid face up on the sewing machine, the border is laid face down and sewn round, using the ½in (1.3cm) seam allowance. The sewn cover is completed by trimming the border length and joining the ends to fit the circular top.

9 The sewn cover is rolled onto the prepared interior by turning it inside out and working the cover over the edges. By turning the pouffe upside-down onto a table surface the sides can be adjusted and eased until they are smooth and wrinkle-free, and the sewn seam is sitting well along the upper edge.

10 A length of linen or nylon twine is stitched along the base of the border fabric using a running stitch. This is sewn about 40mm (1½in) in from the cut edge.

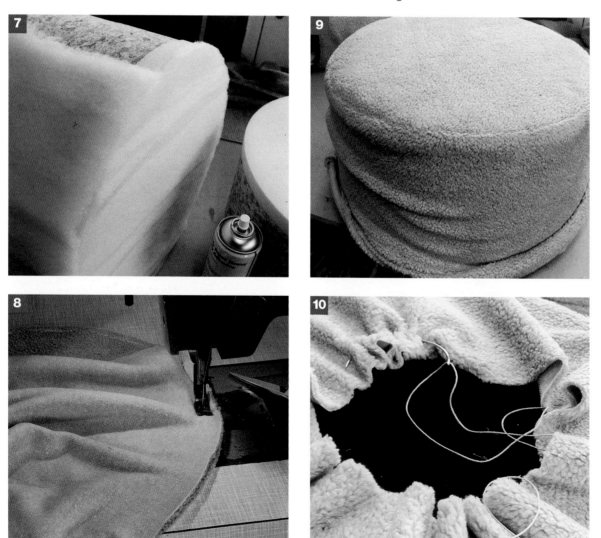

11 The twines can then be pulled tight to gather the whole of the fabric edge into a tightly held circle. The twines can be tied off into a permanent knot, and all the excess twine tucked in, rather than being cut off. If necessary, this will allow for the cover to be removed and refitted again.

12 The raw cut edges of the fabric are then turned under.

13 The completed project.

Project 4
A modern chair

This project is an interesting chair design, very typical of the 1960s, and is one of a set of four. Except for two main cross rails the chair is constructed entirely from laminated timbers, which are formed and curved under pressure. The seat and back supports are also formed and curved to create comfortable sitting shapes.

Materials used

- Combustion modified high resilience foam (40 grade)
- Polyester wadding (2oz (56gm) weight)
- Black cotton, bottom lining
- Spray adhesive
- ⅜in (1cm) staples
- Cream wool/cotton upholstery tweed 118in (3 metres)

Method

1 The triangular-shape chair frame with the upholstered parts removed.

2 Removal of the covering reveals an earlier original plain mustard-colour wool tweed.
A slotted screw system is used to secure the back shape to the keyhole plates in the chair's main frame.

3 A view of the seat underside reveals the four bolting positions. Staple fixings are used throughout the upholstery and taking them all out requires patience and a good deal of time.

4 After sanding and cleaning the new work begins with a ½in (1.3cm) layer of 40 grade seat foam. The foam is trimmed to the seat size and glued in place with spray adhesive. The glue is applied in spots to both surfaces rather than all over the seat area. Spot gluing is adequate and is economical.

5 A second layer of foam is cut oversize by 5cm (2in) and glued in place.
The four ventilation holes in the seat board allow the upholstery to breathe in use.

6 The foam edges are stapled all around the under edge of the seat ply. At the corners the foams are eased into place and squashed flat by the stapling. This produces a smooth curving corner.

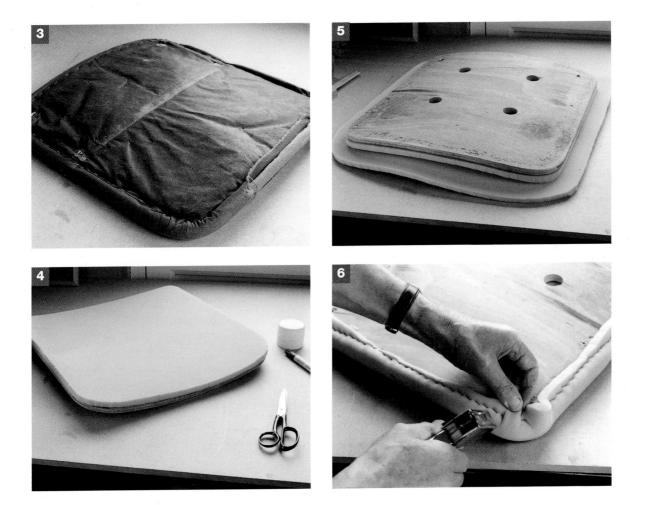

7 With plenty of staples in place, the foams are trimmed off close to the staple line.

8 It is essential that the foams are well glued down across the centre of the seat board, so that they conform to the curving, dished shape of the seat. Working the foams in two separate layers, rather than one thicker layer, produces a well rounded and smooth outline to the seat.

9 Thin layers of polyester fibre are glued over the foams, providing a soft insulator between foam and covering fabric, an essential ingredient in all upholstery foam work.

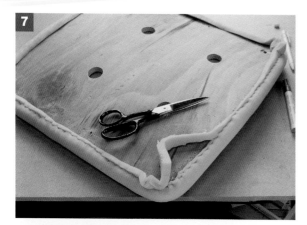

10 After setting the covering fabric in place with temporary tacks, and stretching it well towards the corners, the staple gun is used to complete the fixing. As always, corners are dealt with last by gathering and pleating. The nose of the gun is used to force the fabric into place as each staple is fired.

11 The upholstery fabric is trimmed as close as possible to the staple line. Next, a piece of black cotton lining is cut and fixed to cover the seat base. At this point the staples can be removed from the gun magazine and fresh length painted along their surface with a black marker pen. The staples will then match the black lining colour.

12 The back rest is upholstered with just one layer of ½in (1.3cm) foam and some 2oz (56g) polyester wadding. The inside back and outside back covering is done with one piece of fabric,

well tensioned and stapled. Along the bottom edge of the backrest ply the cover is neatly turned in and finished.

13 The upholstery is positioned and bolted into place to complete this classic chair design of the mid-20th century.

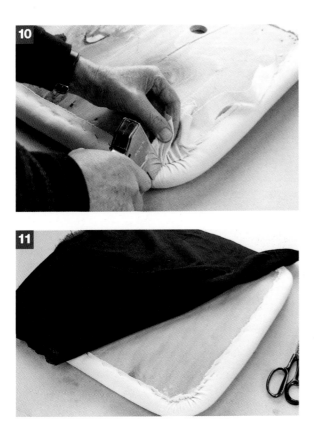

Project 5
A bed headboard, for a single bed

This project introduces the use of sheet materials for upholstery which were developed and first used during the mid-20th century. They were the new materials of the time before synthetic upholstery foams became widely available.

The upholstered headboard allows the upholsterer an opportunity to create almost any design shape and to furnish it using fabrics, colours and trimmings.

2 A layer of new cotton felt is laid over the hair sheet and trimmed with the fingers to the size of the board. As the tissue paper is removed the felt will cling to the hair sheet.

3 Next, prepare the covering fabrics and to make up several metres of piping which are to be used to trim and finish the edges of the headboard. 10 metres of piping strip were marked out and bias cut.

Materials used

- MDF (medium density fibre board)
- Rubberized hair sheet 1in (2.5cm)
- Cotton felt (2½oz (70gm) weight)
- Spray adhesive
- Cotton twist piping cord
- Machine thread (36 size)
- ¼in or ⅜in (7mm or 1cm) tacks
- ⅜in (1cm) staples
- Back-tacking strip
- Calico

Method

1 The project begins with a cut board of ½in (1.3cm) thick MDF, to a single bed width. The height of the board in this case is the same, 36in by 36in (90cm by 90cm). The lower portion of the board is designed to sit behind an average mattress, and so a pencil line is drawn 20cm (8in) up from the bottom edge. This provides a guide-line where the upholstery padding will stop. A piece of 1in (2.5cm) thick rubberized hair is cut to the exact size of the board, finishing at the line and glued into place using a foam spray adhesive.

4 All the strips are joined together (on the sewing machine) to make a continuous length, which has a piping foot fitted.

5 A one metre piece of upholstery fabric is the perfect size for this project. The fabric is centred and temporary tacked in place along the pencil line, pulling up and over the board top, followed by the sides.

6 When the fabric is smooth and tight, stapling begins, with the tacks removed as stapling progresses. The staple line at the board base should be continuously checked with the pencil line.

7 A good edge line is produced by tensioning and stapling the corners as soon as possible. Fixing begins at the centre of the corner. A small square of the fabric is then removed so that the bulk of fabric is reduced.

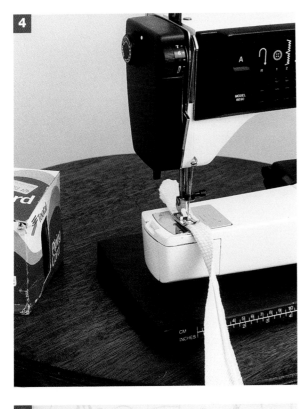

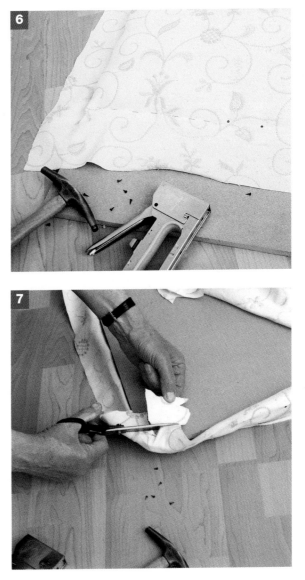

8 Easing and pleating at the corner and some close stapling will produce a clean smooth edge. The outer face edge of the board is kept absolutely clear of the felt filling, as stapling continues.

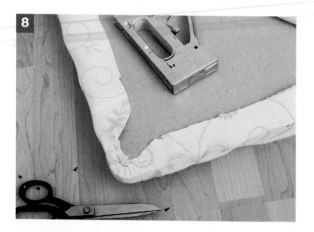

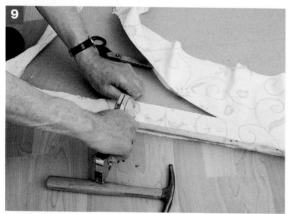

9 Because the covering has been well tensioned towards all the corners, the edges can be eased gently and the stapling and trimming off completed.

10 Three rows of the plain-colour piping are stapled along the outer edge of the board, beginning with the inner row first.

11 The first two rows of piping are stapled to the outer face edge of the board and the third row stapled to the back.

12 The padded area of the headboard is complete.

13 A piece of the plain covering is cut to size and tacked permanently in place on the base staple line.

14 A length of cardboard tacking strip is used to back-tack the fabric in place, with the upper edge of the card strip set just above and hiding the earlier staple line. The fabric is then pulled down and over the lower edges, temporary tacked and made ready for stapling. No filling is used behind the cover panel.

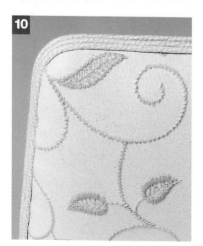

15 The board is laid face down and a piece of calico is carefully stapled to cover over all the previous fixings.

16 Trim out and remove the excess cloth at the corners, before stapling.

17 The completed headboard. A bed headboard can be wall mounted or fixed to a bed base using timber leg supports.

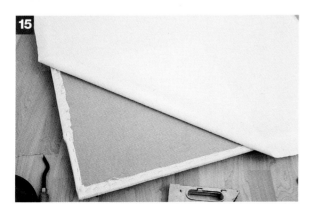

Project 6
A four-fold screen

This project is based on a traditional construction and is upholstered using techniques that were common practice in the 18th and 19th centuries. In those times the screen was a very useful and practical way of providing a draught-proof and screened-off area. Similarly, a screen was often used across a doorway or behind a row of chairs that faced a fireplace. Their uses were universal in all the rooms of a house. In today's centrally heated homes the screen is more a decorative feature and will also serve as a space divider.

Materials used

- A softwood frame
- Heavy grade brown lining paper
- Cotton skin wadding
- Brown and white English webbing
- Gimp pins
- ½in (1.4cm) staples
- Glazed chintz 29ft (9m) 51in 130cm) wide
- Upholstery gimp 62ft (19m)

Method

1 A good-quality softwood is used to construct the framework. Each of the four frames is identical in size, and the shaping pieces at the top are cut to a preferred design and screwed in place. This screen is a medium to small size, making it fairly easy to handle. The height is 5½ft (1.7m) and each fold is 35cm (14in) wide. The timber rails are all 1½in by ¾in (4cm by 2cm) thick.

2 Each of the frames is lined with a good-quality strong brown paper. The paper is cut to size and glued with a spray adhesive to all the rails on both sides of the frames. When the adhesive is perfectly dry and the paper well fixed, shrink the paper by painting on water with a brush or sponge. Making sure that only the unsupported areas between the rails are dampened, and the glued areas remain dry.

3 When the frames are perfectly dry and the paper has become drum tight, the upholstery work can begin. Care needs to be taken not to damage the linings, as a half-layer of skin wadding is cut and applied to one side of the frames. This can be held secure with a few small tacks or staples.

4 A glazed cotton chintz was chosen for the face side of the screen. On printed fabrics, labelling is always helpful and should be noted in case ironing or cleaning is required.

5 Three pieces could be cut from the fabric width, and a fourth from another length. The cut pieces were numbered and kept labelled throughout the upholstery work to ensure matching of the design.

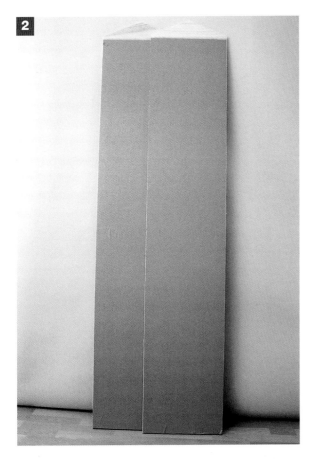

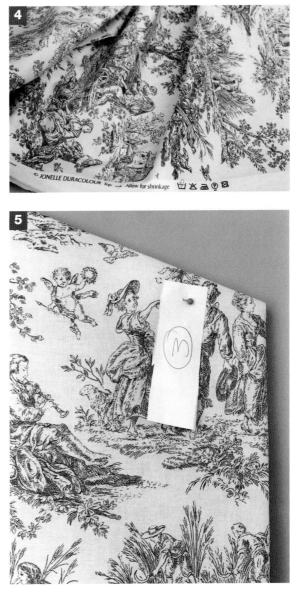

6 The four covering fabric pieces are temporary tacked at the edges of the screen frames and set in position with a little tension. As stapling continues the temporary tacks are removed.

7 A plain putty colour glazed chintz was selected for the reverse side and this is positioned and stapled with another half-thickness of skin wadding. Each of the corners is neatly folded and stapled. Trim off the excess accurately.

8 When the covering of the frames is complete, the six hinging strips are cut, along with three lengths of best-quality webbing, three strips 2in (5cm) wide, of each of the face fabric and the reverse fabric.

9 The webbing strips are trimmed to reduce the width to 1½in (4cm). The upholstered panels are joined together in pairs, using the face fabric and the webbing, ensuring that the panels are aligned.

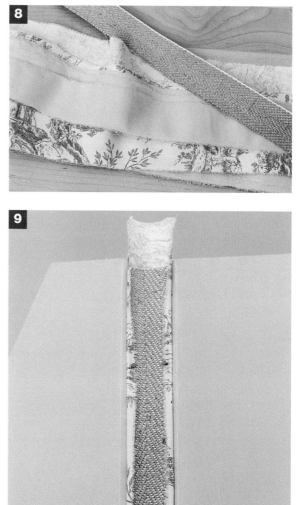

10 When the hinging pieces are set on and temporary tacked with fine tacks or gimp pins, the ends at the top and bottom are folded back and fixed.

11 With the pair of panels folded together, the tacking is made permanent.

12 Fabric matching and the alignment of the panels should be checked regularly.

13 When both pairs of panels are hinged together then the remaining strips can be fitted.

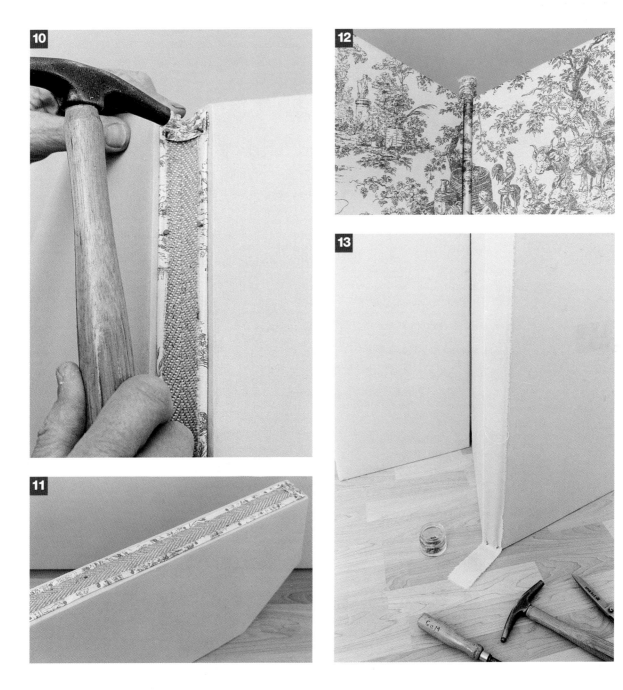

14 13mm gimp pins make an ideal fixing, spaced about 1¼in to 1½in (3 to 4cm) apart, with fabric turned in and the pins set back from the edges. When brass hinges are preferred, they can be fitted at this stage, before the second covering is fixed.

15 The two completed pairs of panels can then be joined together by hinging the centre edges. Align the screen by standing it on a level floor before carrying out the final hinging and fixing. As an alternative fixing ½in (1.3cm) staples were used to complete the final hinge.

16 Begin fixing the gimp or braid at the bottom of the screen, with the ends of the trimming turned in and glued and also gimp pinned, to ensure a permanent fixing. About 19 metres of gimp were used to complete the trimming of all the edges.

17 The corners are all inspected and where

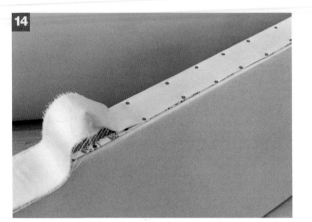

necessary extra matching gimp pins added.

18 The completed screen.

Project 7
An Edwardian mahogany corner chair

In this project a traditional squab cushion is produced for the seat of this unusual chair. The chair is made entirely from mahogany with some inlay decoration. The solid timber seat forms the main construction in the Windsor style.

Materials used

- Tarpaulin 14oz (390g)
- Calico 5oz (150g) quality
- Curled hair mixture
- Cotton wadding 52oz (145g)
- Mattress twine
- Piping cord
- Machine thread 36oz poly/cotton
- Cotton repp 39in (1m) 55in (140cm) wide
- Size 22 buttons

Method

1 The seat has been scooped out or adzed to provide some comfort.

2 Begin by cutting a paper pattern to represent the shape and outline of the new squab. Two pieces of calico are cut to the seat size, plus an allowance of ½in (1.3cm) for sewing and the centres marked.

3 The border strips are cut from 14oz (390gm) tarpaulin 2½in (6cm) wide. These provide the stiff outer edge to the squab interior. With the calico panel face up and the border face down the two are machine sewn together, very close to the folded edges.

4 The joins on the borders are arranged at the back of the case and the main seam lines are marked as a guide, on both the calico and the border tarpaulin.

5 The under panel of calico is then sewn onto the squab case, leaving a filling gap along the whole of the back edge.

6 Commencing at the front of the case the squab is tightly filled to a good firm density, working gradually back and pushing the hair filling into place. The palm of the hand is used to control the height and thickness and stop the case from ballooning as the density increases. 2½lb (1.1kg) of hair is used to fill the case.

15 The completed interior is checked for size and shape. A reduction in size is inevitable and can be compensated for when cutting the calico panels.

16 The next stage is to fill over the tufting stitches with soft wads of cotton, and produce an even surface. Two or three layers of soft cotton wadding are cut oversize to wrap the interior, and some long strips to line the edges of the cover.

17 The upholstery fabric is cut to a template size with a sewing allowance of ½in (1.3cm) all around. A border strip is also cut 2⅜in (6cm) wide by the width of the fabric which is 55in (140cm). Three metres of piping is made up in preparation for making up the squab covering.

18 The assembly of the cover begins with the piping being sewn around the two cover panels. An overlapping scarf joint is used to finish the piping. Here the piping cord is cut out of both ends before the overlap is made. The piping is snipped at each corner to allow it to turn around the corner shapes.

19 The border strips are sewn to the piped panels and the corners are carefully located so that they are vertically opposite.

20 The underside panel is left open along three sides of the cover case so that the squab interior can be easily located into the cover and more wadding added where needed. The border is closed and pinned to the piped edge.

21 The border is turned in and slip stitched to the underside of the piping. When the stitches are kept small the seam will be almost invisible.

22 Seven size 22 buttons are arranged in a pattern which suits the squab shape then threaded on to lengths of twine and their positions marked with chalk.

23 Beginning in the centre the buttons are positioned and the twines pulled through to the underside. With the squab turned over, seven more buttons are threaded on to one of the twines and each is pulled down with a slip knot. All the buttons are tightened down and a half hitch is used to tie them off. The surplus twine is snipped off and the ends tucked under each button.

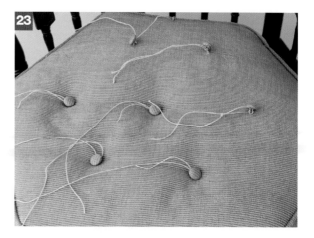

24 All the buttons are pulled to an even depth to complete the squab.

Project 8
A walnut writing chair, 19th century

Sometimes called corner chairs, this project is a mid-Victorian version of an early 18th-century design. The seat has been upholstered several times, and the existing covering fabric is a cut wool moquette which can be dated at around 1920–40.

Materials used

- Black and white English webbing
- 14oz (390g) hessian
- Curled hair mixture
- Linen scrim
- Calico
- Cotton skin wadding
- Mattress twine
- ½in (1.3cm) and ⅜in (1cm) tacks
- Raw silk fabric 39in (1m)
- Scroll gimp 79in (2m)
- Antique on brass upholstery nails

Method

1 A well-made chair in solid walnut with a shell carving on the front cabriole leg. The seat upholstery has collapsed and is in desperate need of some restoration. A braid is used to finish the covering and runs all around the seat edge.

2 The design of the frame is attractive and generously proportioned.

3 The chair seat is webbed using English black and white webbing and 1.3cm (½in) improved tacks, in a three by three formation.

4 A good quality 14oz (390g) hessian is tacked and stretched to produce a firm platform.

5 Tacking commences at the back of the seat and the hessian is pulled well to the front with tacks set along the centre of the rails. The platform is completed by turning back the edges and tacking a second time.

6 The bridle ties to hold the stuffing are put in using an overlapping back stitch. Here the czzhamfered edge, which is prepared for the scrim tacking, can be seen clearly. A first stuffing of curled hair is put in around the edges, the front two edges are stuffed more densely to create a sloping seat.

7 Along the front edges of the seat, each handful of hair is given a twist and fold, before being pushed under the ties. This creates a firm nose of hair which is then set under the tie along the very edge of the rail front. This is an ideal build in preparation for a stitched edge front, and is a useful technique that can be used with animal hair fillings.

8 A linen scrim is cut to size and temporary tacked over the hair first stuffing, along the two back edges the scrim is turned in.

9 Using a mattress twine and a two-point bayonette needle a pattern for the stuffing ties is stabbed into the scrim. Stuffing tie patterns should follow the shape of the seat whenever possible and should be kept well back from the outer edges.

10 The stuffing ties are in the form of a running stitch and go down through the seat to catch the webbings or hessian in the platform. Before tying off, the ties are tightened down to compress the stuffing a little.

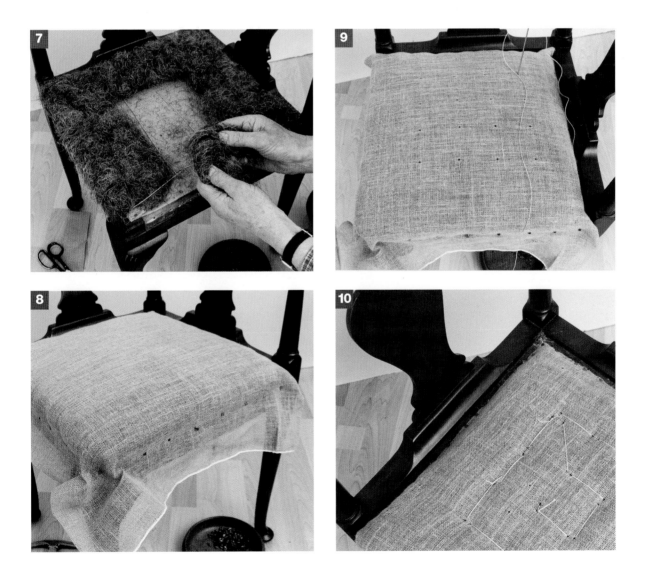

11 The noses of edge stuffing are teased out a little to produce an evenly filled edge, and the scrim is rolled under and tacked into the chamfered rail edge. At the front corner the scrim is carefully set around the edge and is folded and pleated, using the fingers and a regulator. The corner should be firm and well filled with hair before tacking down.

12 Excess scrim is trimmed away at the corner before tacking down with ⅜in (1cm) or ¼in (7m) m fine tacks. When the scrim tacking is complete the whole seat edge should be well regulated, to firm the edge a little more and even out the feel of the edges.

13 To produce a stitched edge a row of blind stitches is put in along the front of the seat very close to the tacks. The blind stitch draws the hair filling to the edge and begins to build a firm foundation for the top stitching. Blind stitching needs to be pulled very firmly and a leather glove can be used to protect the fingers from the fine twine. The knot is formed by winding the twine twice around the needle as it emerges from the scrim. Again, the twine is then pulled very tightly.

14 At intervals of about every sixth stitch, a locking stitch is made to hold the row firmly and stop the previous stitches loosening.

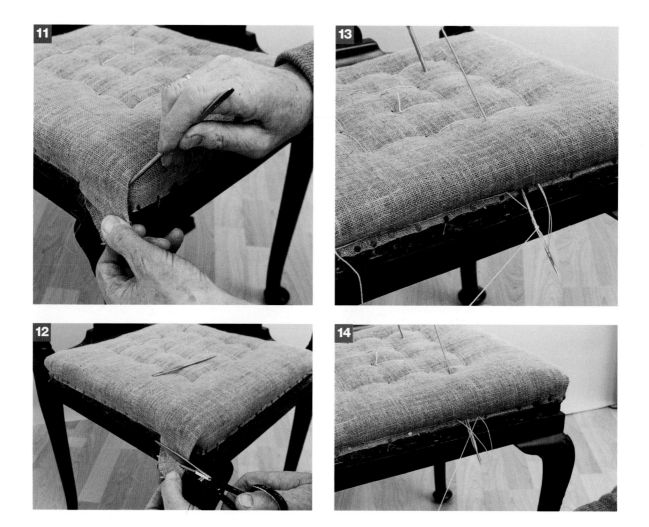

15 When a length of twine runs out, A new length is started with a slipknot, and before tightening, the end of the previous twine is wound in twice. After tightening down the slipknot the old twine end can be snipped off.

16 A second row of blind stitching is put in just above the first, producing a good firm edge. After regulating again, the roll at the top of the edge is formed with a row of top stitching.

17 Top stitches should be close and kept as straight as possible, in this case the thread lines of the scrim can be followed, to produce a straight line of stitches.

18 To reinforce the front corner, an extra stitch is added in the form of a mitre, pulled tightly using a slipknot and tied off below the edge.

19 Bridle ties are put into the top of the seat and the second stuffing of hair is teased into a thin layer, stopping just short of the stitched edge.

20 The first covering is a calico, pulled tight and temporary tacked all round the seat. The front corner is dealt with by fixing with four tacks, hammered in permanently, and a square of the calico trimmed away.

21 Two pleats in a 'V' formation form the completed front corner.

22 With great care, using a fine-head hammer, the tacking around the two back edges is made permanent. The right- and left-hand corners are then formed with a single pleat.

23 When the tacking is completed and made permanent a full layer of cotton skin wadding is trimmed and laid over the seat.

24 The seat is covered in a plain cloth of silk and wool mixture. The setting on with temporary tacks is dealt with in the same way as the calico. The

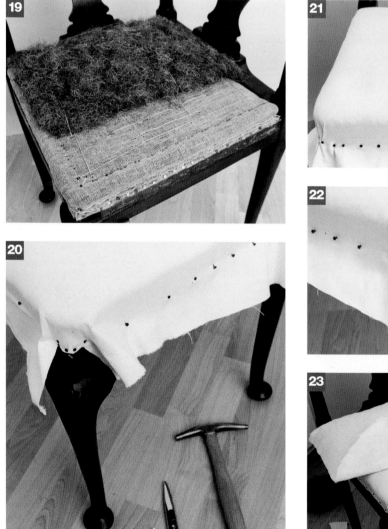

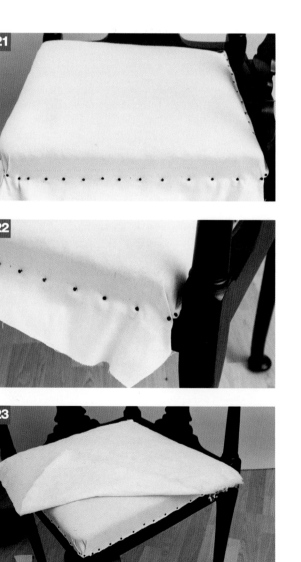

selvedge of the fabric is along the right-hand edge and the textured surface grain, which is typical of silk fabrics, runs across the seat, side to side.

25 After temporary tacking the sides all around the seat, the corner is pulled and set with three tacks. The fabric is then tightened and plenty of tacks added, before the corner is trimmed and pleated in.

26 With the tacking made permanent the seat is ready for trimming and decoration. A matching upholstery gimp is chosen and is glued in place with a clear fabric adhesive. Antique brass nails are spaced at 3cm (1¼in) intervals along the braid, a method often used by French upholsterers for chair decoration. The nail positions are marked on to the frame using white chalk.

27 As nailing progresses care has to be taken

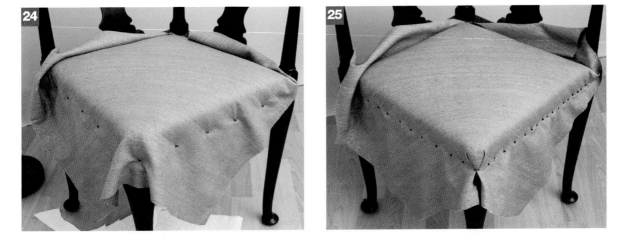

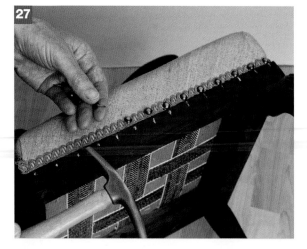

with their positioning, each nail guided in using the fingers, and gentle taps with the hammer. Adjustments to line up the row of nails can be made with a nail punch. Nailing around the back of the seat requires care and patience to avoid damaging the show-wood edges.

28 Two brass nails set close together enhance the front corner.

29 The completed chair.

Project 9
A sprung stool

T his stool with a sprung seat was manufactured about the middle of the 20th century and has Queen Ann-style cabriole legs made from beech that is stained and polished to a dark colour. The age of the stool can be confirmed by the general appearance and the upholstery materials that were used, which all appear to be original. It was also noticeable that there were no other tack holes in the frame, other than the original fixings. Although not originally sprung, the stool is an ideal candidate on which to demonstrate the processes involved in springing a small seat.

Materials used

- Black and white English webbing
- Double cone springs 10swg
- 14oz (390g) tarpaulin
- Coir fibre (ginger) 3lb (1.4kg)
- Grey curled hair mixture ¾lb (0.4kg)
- Jute scrim 9oz (250g)
- Calico
- Cotton skin wadding
- Waxed slipping thread
- Mattress twine No 3 and No 5
- Black cotton lining
- Cotton/silk upholstery weave 39in (1m)
- Cotton velour half metre
- Flanged cord 118in (3m)
- Gimp pins
- ½in (1.3cm) staples
- ½in (1.3cm) and 10mm tacks

Method

1 A thin thumb roll or dug roll formed the original edging with a stuffing of Algerian grass fibre.

111

2 A handmade seat tapestry has adorned the stool since it was first made and certainly shows its age.

3 The frame has corner blocks fitted, which act as a brace, and the rails have a good thickness of timber.

4 The stool is webbed with black and white English webbing on the underside, in a four and three pattern, interwoven. ½in (1.3cm) staples were used to fix the webbings. Tacks have been used throughout the rest of the project. The use of long staples is well suited to the fixing of webbing in a frame of some age. The five springs are the double cone type and are 4in (1cm) high with a wire gauge of 10swg. If the seat was intended for constant heavy use a 9swg spring would be a better choice, producing a firmer seat. All the upper knots on the springs are positioned facing an opposite diagonal corner to give a balanced unit.

5 Using a curved springing needle and No 5 twine the springs are sewn in to the webs, with three knots to each.

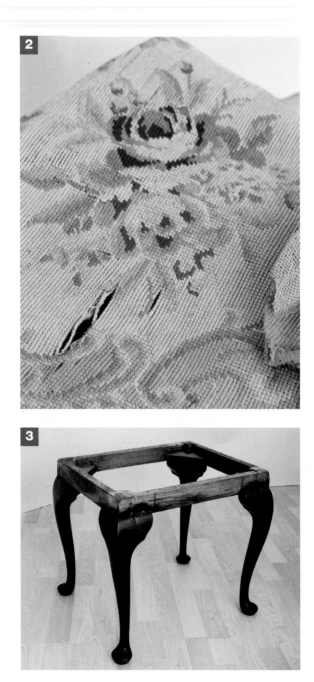

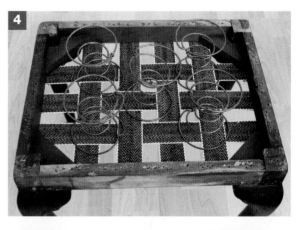

6 The springs are lashed with a laid cord and the lashing fixed by two ⅝in (1.6cm) improved tacks. The sequence for lashing is three rows back to front, followed by two rows side to side, and finally a diagonal row from leg to leg.

7 The springs are covered with a good 14oz (390g) tarpaulin, and the needle and twine used again to tie the tops of the springs at three points to each. A No 5 linen mattress twine is used to tie springs to webbings and to hessians and tarpaulins.

8 Bridle ties are back stitched around the edge of the seat and three rows across the seat in preparation for the first stuffing. The stuffing is a ginger coconut fibre, which has been curled and processed for upholstery.

9 Measurements are taken for the scrim covering from the bottom of the seat rails.

10 A thread is pulled out from the centre of the scrim to provide a centre line and help to keep it straight when tacked on. Using a regulator the stuffing tie positions are stabbed into the scrim. These are kept well in from the edges by about 5in (12.5cm).

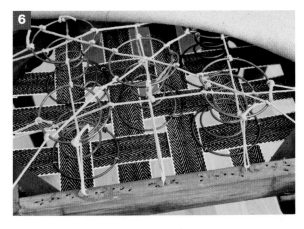

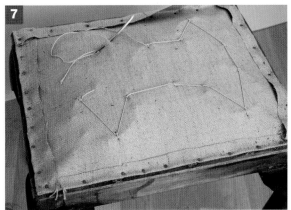

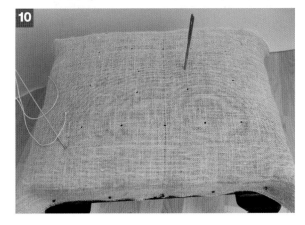

11 Putting the stuffing ties in begins with a slip-knot. All the ties are in the form of a running stitch and are caught inside the stool by the tarpaulin. The stitches do not go down to the webbing or the springs. The ties are tightened to compress the filling a little, and then tied off at the seat centre.

12 Beginning at any of the four edges, the scrim is trimmed off below the tack line and the temporary tacks removed.

13 The scrim is rolled back and some more filling added to firm the edge.

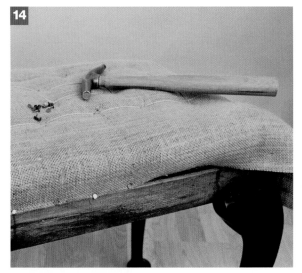

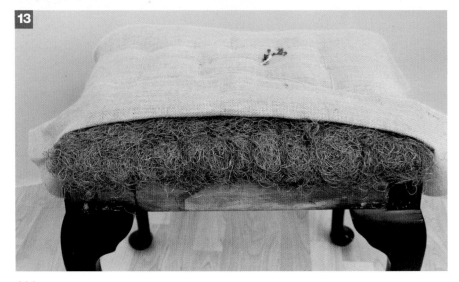

14 The edges are worked one at a time, filled with extra stuffing and the scrim rolled under and tacked to the edge chamfer. The edge should feel very full and remain square and upright. The regulator is now used to help firm the edge and work more stuffing into it.

15 Making the edges begins with a fine mattress twine and a two-point needle, pushed from the tack line at about 45 degrees and up through the scrim. As the eye of the needle appears, the needle is swung to the right and pushed down to emerge from the scrim, about 1½in (3.8cm) to the left of the first entry.

16 A slipknot is then made and the twine pulled hard, both away from the stool and along the stool edge. As the slipknot is tightened the stuffing caught by the twine will be moved into the edge. This technique has been used for some two centuries in upholstery and bedding making.

17 The stitching continues in the same way, entering the scrim at an angle, and returning as the eye of the needle appears. The needle is moved back down to the left of the first entry, taking in some of the filling.

18 With the needle halfway out of the scrim, a knot is formed by two turns around the needle anti-clockwise. The needle is withdrawn and the twine given a very hard pull, again away from and along the stool. Regulating the edge continuously as stitching progresses is essential.

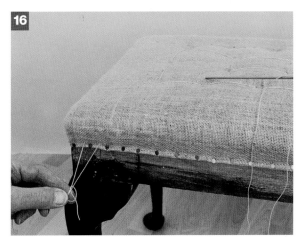

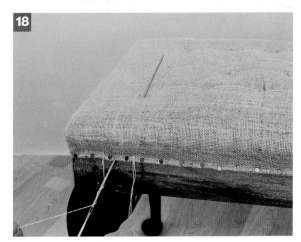

19 Every six stitches or so a locking stitch can be made; take the left twine over the needle then the right twine over the needle, withdraw the needle and pull tight.

20 The edge of the seat is made with one blind row of stitching and two top rows. The first top row forms a roll about 1in (2.5cm) thick. When the twine runs out, it is linked into the slipknot of the new twine, pulled tight and trimmed off.

21 The second row of top stitches cuts the first roll approximately in half to create a sharp edge.

22 The roll is pinched with the fingers as the twine is pulled. This helps to form the edge and reduces the strain on the twine.

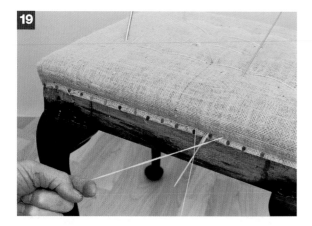

23 The second stuffing of hair gives the stool a dome shape and adds some softness. Nylon-headed skewers are used to set the calico onto the edge, and the hair is tucked inside the roll edge.

24 The skewers are set at an angle to the edge so that the calico can be held very tight. The calico edges are trimmed, leaving enough to turn in.

25 As the calico is turned in and repinned it is stretched tight again.

26 The calico is slip stitched to the outer edge of the scrim roll.

27 Two layers of skin wadding are trimmed to fit the top of the stool exactly. At the same time the covering fabric is measured a little oversize and cut.

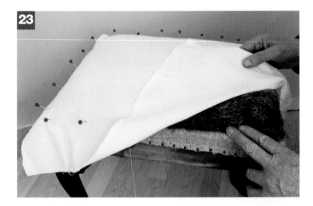

28 The fabric is treated exactly as for the calico, turned in and pinned to the outer edge.

29 Plenty of skewers are needed to hold the fabric, in preparation for slip stitching with a matching dark colour slipping thread.

30 A flanged upholstery cord was chosen for the stool edge, and is pinned in place. The ends of the cord are cut and separated to form the join by overlapping and laying the yarns together. The join needs to be well pinned.

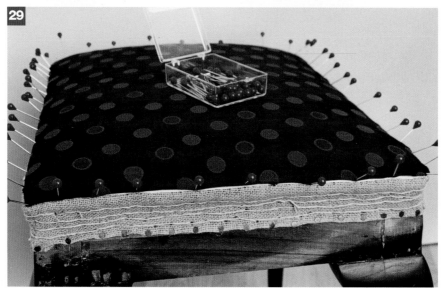

31 A cotton velvet was cut for the border. Two widths of the velvet 6in (15cm) wide are turned in and pinned to the flanged cord. A few temporary tacks are used to hold the border along the stool under-edge. A matching red waxed slipping thread is chosen for the sewing work. The border is slip stitched to the fabric top by passing the needle through and under the cord after each stitch.

32 Each stitch is pulled tight as the cord is neatly trapped. Two of the corners have joins which are dealt with after the border is filled.

33 When the stitching is completed the border is filled with two layers of skin wadding, folded to make four thickness.

34 The border fabric is eased smoothly down and temporary tacked, and the cuts made at each leg, to allow for turning the velvet along the edges of the legs. Matching gimp pins hold the border in place at the leg corners and the border corners are turned in and slip stitched to complete the covering.

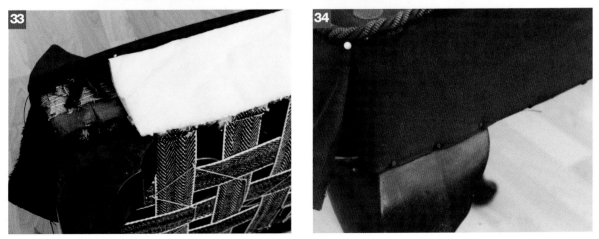

35 A black cotton lining cloth is tacked to the underside as a dust cover, this is advisable when a seat is sprung.

36 The completed stool.

Project 10
A balloon-back dining chair (c1870)

The 19th century saw the development of many new styles of which the balloon back was a very dominant one. Great numbers of variations appeared between 1840 and 1880 with cabriole legs and turned legs. It was a style that persisted over several decades. Our project is one of a set of six and is made from walnut. Its condition is reasonably good considering its age.

Materials and equipment

- Brown and white English webbing 5cm wide
- Hessian 14oz (390g)
- Curled hair (80/20 pig and cow)
- Jute scrim 9oz (250g)
- Cotton calico
- Skin wadding (32oz (900g) quality)
- Mattress twine No 3 and No 5
- Embroidery thread
- Poly/cotton machine thread 36
- Clear fabric adhesive
- Black cotton lining
- ½in (1.3cm), ⅜in(1cm) and ¼in (7mm)
- Gimp pins

Method

1 Five metres of damask with a large repeated pattern and 14 metres of braid were used on this set of chairs.

2 The English brown and white webbings were fixed with ½in (1.3cm) improved tacks in a four and three pattern, interwoven.

3 A good 14oz (390g) hessian was stretched hand-tight over the webbings to complete the seat support.

4 At the leg corners the hessian is cut from its corner to the corner of the leg. This allows the cloth to sit well for tacking.

5 Bridle ties are put in around the inner edge of the seat and across the centre, with a curved stitching needle.

6 A good layer of ginger fibre is tied in to a thickness of 2in (5cm). The edges are filled first with three small handfuls pushed into each tie. Coir fibre makes a good first stuffing and produces a firm seat, ideal for dining chair upholstery. Time taken to fill the edges well to a good density saves having to add more later.

7 When the seat stuffing is complete a 9oz (250g) jute scrim is measured for and cut. Measurements are taken from the bottom edge of each side of the seat.

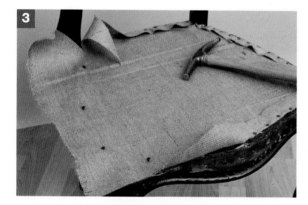

8 Temporary tacking with ⅜in (1cm) fine tacks begins at the back of the chair seat.

9 The thread lines are kept straight and square as the scrim is temporary tacked all round. The scrim is folded back at each leg and the cuts are made up to within ¼in (1cm) of the leg. This allows some tuck away for the scrim.

10 Trim away the excess scrim with enough to turn in, around each leg.

11 Work begins on the edges, with more filling to be added for firmness.

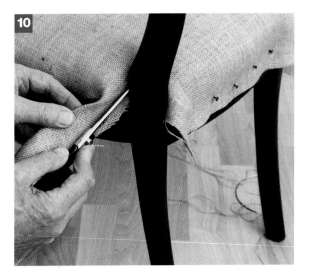

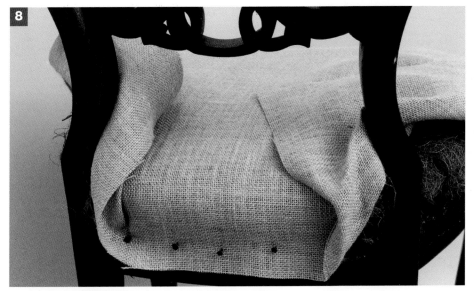

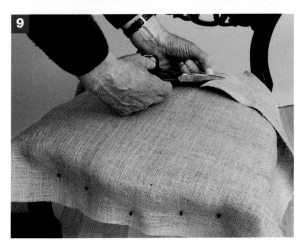

12 Squeeze the edge to test the firmness and roll in the scrim under the stuffing. On a chair seat of this shape, where there are no straight edges, the upholstery has to be continually checked for shape to ensure that it follows the frame curves. The thread lines on the scrim will drift downwards towards the corners.

13 Here the scrim threads drop towards the back leg. Tack permanently into the shamfer when the edge stuffing is firm. A good overhang is essential if the edge is to follow the frame line. The corners are built by temporary tacking at the centre and pushing the stuffing in to a firm point.

14 The scrim is trimmed leaving enough to turn in and make the corner. With two very small pleats set at the corner, the tacking is completed. The edges are well regulated to bring the stuffing out and over the tack line. Plenty of tacks are added before stitching begins.

15 The blind stitch begins at the left-hand back corner of the seat. A slipknot is made using the two-point needle. The blind stitch progresses as the twine is wound twice round the needle to form the knot. The row of blind stitches is kept very close to the tack line.

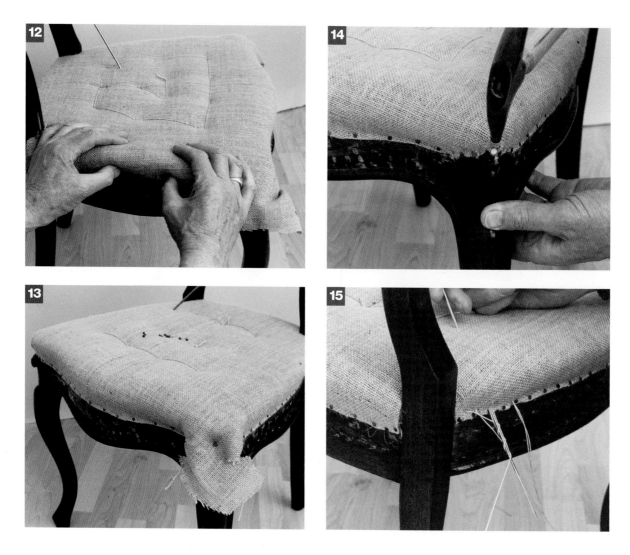

16 Turn the chair on its side, to check the edge line produced by the blind stitching.

17 A row of top stitching forms the edge roll around the seat.

18 The bridle ties for the second stuffing begin at the back of the seat. The more scrim that is taken in by the needle the more the ties will flex and

tighten when the stuffing is inserted. Ties should run around the outer edge and across the centre and be approximately the width of the hand in length.

19 The second stuffing of curled hair is tied in with a slight centre crown and stopped just inside the stitched edge. No hair stuffing should be allowed to creep over the outer edges. The comfort of the seat is built in to the second stuffing. Victorian chairs tend to be given a more rounded outline than those designs made in the preceding periods, at the end of the 18th century and the beginning of the 19th century.

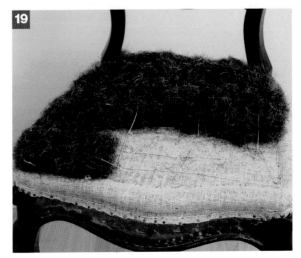

20 A piece of calico is cut a little oversize in preparation for the first covering. Calico is used to produce shape and outline and is a cloth that will withstand a good amout of tensioning.

21 The first fixing is at the back of the seat with ⅜in (1cm) fine tacks, followed by firm pulling to the seat front. The stitched edge should then begin to show as a sharp outline below the calico. The calico is then well tensioned over the seat sides. Two tacks placed close together will hold the calico and avoid the possibility of tearing.

22 Plenty of temporary tacks are added all around the seat sides, about halfway down the rails. The front corners can then be dealt with, and set with three tacks before trimming. Two small tight pleats in a 'V' pattern are put in above the front legs.

23 Excess calico is trimmed at the back leg corners and the regulator is used to tuck away the cut edges.

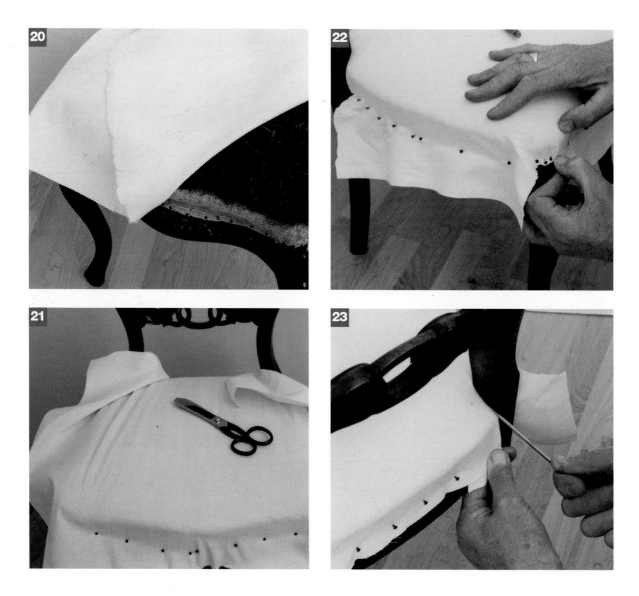

24 On a curving seat, a strong pull is needed to clean out and stretch the calico smoothly. The pull is diagonal and down at the same time.

25 Skin wadding is split to produce a large piece for the seat and at least two layers should be used. The wadding is trimmed to fit well over the edge and cover the tacking line.

26 The upholstery fabric is carefully measured and cut with a central motif for each seat. Two pieces could be cut from the 55in (140cm) width with some wastage for the pattern matching, so that each chair of the set could be identical. The fabric is centred and temporary tacked in place using the same sequence as for the calico. Plenty of fine ⅜in (1cm) or ¼in (7mm) tacks are used along the lower edges of the rails, and set close to the show-wood beadings.

27 When the tacks have been made permanent, the cover is trimmed carefully along the show-wood edges.

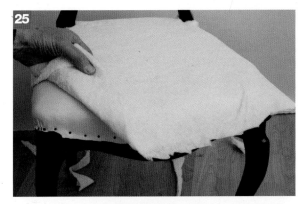

28 The braid is glued around the seat edges with a clear fabric adhesive. At the leg corners a mitre is formed by folding and gluing the braid and fixing a matching gimp pin into each mitre. The braid is temporarily held in place with pins as the glue sets. The braiding is completed at the back of the chair, and is finally trimmed, turned in and gimp pinned up to the leg.

29 Five small 1.8cm (⅝in) diameter tufts were made to decorate the seat. These are easily produced using a tufting stick and some embroidery thread blended with some strong red machine thread. The blended yarns are wound over the stick seven winds forward and seven winds back, and then tightly tied across the centre with three winds of machine thread. The tufts are removed from the stick and the cross winds tied very tight and knotted.

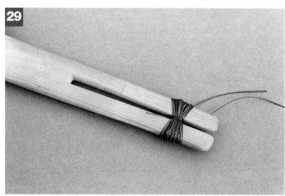

30 The tightness of the cross winds produces a spread of the yarns and a floral shape is formed.

31 A length of mattress twine is used to tie the tufts into the seat.

32 A toggle of calico is used to hold the slip knots and set the tufts to an even depth in the seat. These are then tied off permanently with a double hitch. Research has shown that balloon-back chairs in the early Victorian period were occasionally decorated in this way.

33 A black cotton lining cloth is fitted as a dust cover using 7mm (¼in) fine tacks.

34 The completed chair.

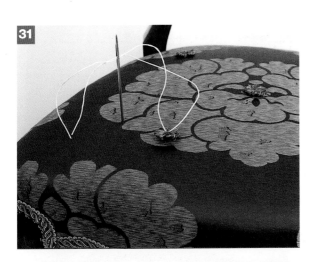

Project 11
A set of Louis XVI-style oval-back salon chairs

This project uses a variety of techniques for the restoration of the upholstery. Emphasis is placed on the reuse of the original materials as much as possible and their integration into the rebuilding process.

It demonstrates some of the possibilities, by combining the old and the new, and shows the beginner that it is not always necessary to throw out old and original materials when they are of good quality and can be cleaned and reused.

Our project is one of a set of 19th-century salon chairs made from ebonized beech in the French style. The frames have been carefully restored and finished ready for the upholstery.

At the back-leg seat joints, blocks have been fitted to provide a seat level and a finishing platform for the upholstery materials, which is typical of French upholstered seating design. All the original materials taken from the chairs are English, and of good quality.

Method
1 A strong chair frame of nice proportions with the tacking surfaces in good condition.

Materials and equipment

- Brown and white English webbing
- Jute tarpaulin
- 10oz (280g) hessian
- Washed and carded horse hair
- Skin wadding
- Calico
- Mattress twine No 5, No 3 and No 2
- ½in (1.3cm) staples
- ⅜in (1cm) and ¼in (7mm) fine tacks
- Slipping thread
- Original horse hair pads

2 The rewebbing of the seat begins with centre web first.

3 Using ½in (1.3cm) staples a pattern of five and four webs, interwoven, is used.

4 At the leg blocks the tarpaulin is cut to take it round and on to the rails. A 'V' cut is made to the width of the blocks. The tarpaulin is stretched and

stapled with ½in (1.3cm) staples. The use of staples for the foundation work is an option, and was chosen as a less intrusive fixing.

5 A scrim covering put in by a previous upholsterer, is removed by cutting all the stitching.

6 The original scrim is revealed and the original stitchwork, now more than a hundred years old.

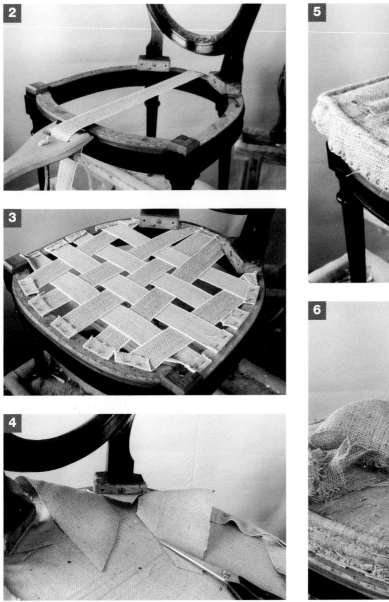

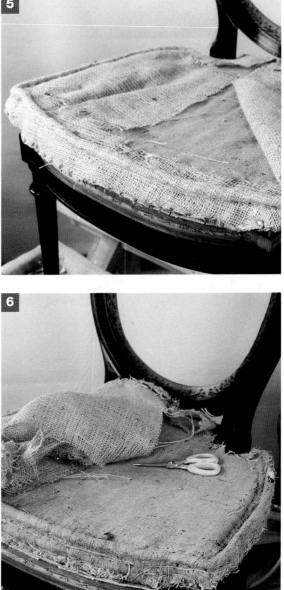

7 The seat is measured for its new scrim and a piece 29½in (75cm) square is cut.

8 After a thorough vacuum cleaning, the seat pad is replaced with an additional layer of washed horse hair laid into the seat first.

9 The linen scrim is set in place, beginning at the back of the seat.

10 Using ⅜in (1cm) tacks, the scrim is set tight with temporary tacks. At the back leg blocks the scrim is cut to fit neatly around the legs and temporary tacked to the blocks.

11 The stuffing tie pattern is stabbed into the scrim and the tying in begins, following the shape of the seat outline.

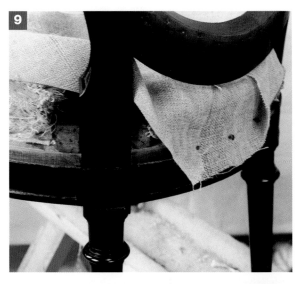

12 The linen scrim is trimmed back, leaving just enough for turning. The seat front is dealt with first.

13 The regulator is used to hold the scrim onto the edge chamfer as tacking begins.

14 When all sides have been temporary tacked, the corners are made by tacking the scrim round the seat front this tack is made permanent. A vertical cut is made to take out some excess scrim.

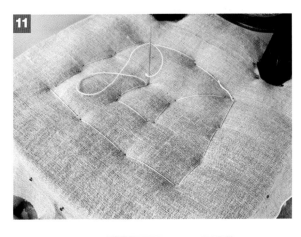

15 A portion of the scrim is cut away and the corner is turned in and pleated with a single pleat.

16 More excess scrim is cut away from the bottom edge, near to the tack line and the corner is completed by temporary tacking.

17 Plenty of tacks are added along the chamfer edge and the tacking on the leg block is made permanent.

18 At the back of the seat the scrim fixing is dealt with, combining the use of the hammer and regulator. As tacking progresses, all the chamfer tacks remain temporary.

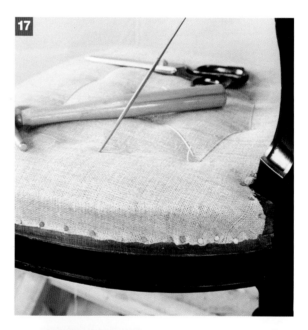

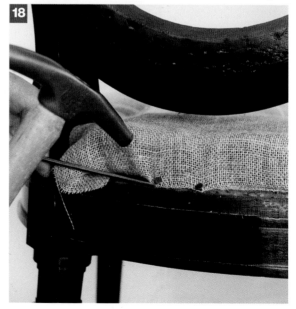

19 At each end of the back rail the scrim is turned in and fixed to the leg blocks. The tack stitch, used to secure the seat pad and hold it well out to the edges, is a very old and early type of stitch developed in the 18th century by upholders. Using the temporary tacks the stitch begins by fixing the twine to the first tack, and hammering the tack in.

20 The needle enters the scrim alongside the first tack at an angle of approximately 45 degrees.

21 The needle does a blind stitch and is returned as soon as the eye appears above the seat surface, at an angle to emerge alongside the next but one tack.

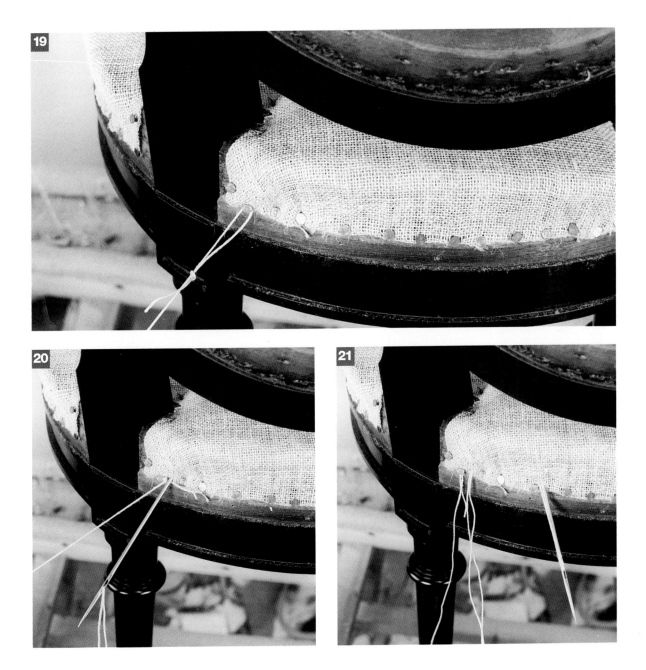

22 The needle is placed somewhere safe and the twine pulled and wound round the tack. The tack can then be hammered home to secure the stitch.

23 The tack stitch progresses as every other tack is used to hold the twine after it is tensioned into the pad.

24 When necessary the pad can be eased to the edge with the regulator, to assist with the positioning. Pulling the twine to move the filling and tighten the edge has to be judged carefully, over-pulling should be avoided.

25 When the tack stitching is completed the twines will be almost invisible. A top stitch is now worked around the seat to reinforce and sharpen the edge. This is put in along the same stitch line as the original top stitch, and can be located easily with the fingers.

26 A shaping stitch is put in at the front, above the inside leg point, to pull the stitched edge back in line with the frame on both sides of the chair.

27 A new top stuffing of some old washed and carded horse hair is added to the seat and tied in with bridle ties. The new calico covering is temporary tacked and pulled tight, to recreate the seat shape.

28 The corners are tightly pleated and tacked down and the calico is turned in and made permanent around the leg blocks.

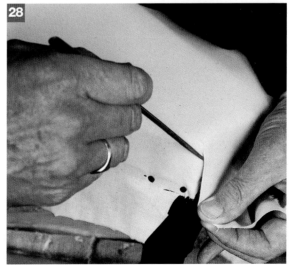

29 The back upholstery begins with a new foundation of webbing and 14oz (390g) hessian. ⅜in (1cm) staples were used for this purpose.

30 The hessian is well tensioned vertically but not horizontally, so that the curve of the back upholstery is maintained.

31 After a thorough vacuum cleaning, the original back pad is fitted in place. This type of upholstery is often referred to as the dead stuffing and is created to form a well for the main stuffing.

32 A piece of new scrim is stitched into the well using a running stitch to attach it to the hessian base.

33 Temporary tacking begins in the rebated edge of the back with fine tacks. In curved upholstery it is necessary to work the cloth in gradually by tacking in between the previous tacks and then again in between, until all the scrim is secured. Some ⅜in (1cm) and some ¼in (7mm) tacks were used. The tack stitch is used to secure the edge, working along the alternate tacks with a curved stitching needle.

34 The holes around the scrim show the progression of the tack stitch and the point at which the needle is returned. Here, two more stitches will bring the needle back to the starting point.

35 The same 15cm (6in) curved stitching needle is used to put in the top stitch, around the edge. A fine mattress twine is used to work the top stitch through the original stitch line.

36 The completed well and top stitching.

37 After thorough cleaning the original horse hair stuffing is laid into the well.

38 A layer of new skin wadding is cut to fit the shape of the edge.

39 The new calico lining is trimmed and turned in and tightly skewered along the stitched edge.

40 The calico is slip stitched with a 3in (7.5cm) slipping needle and some waxed linen thread.

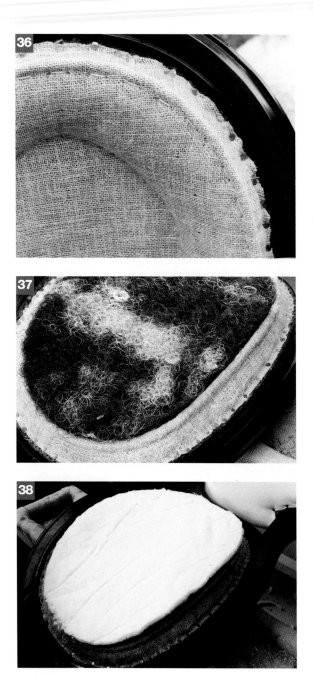

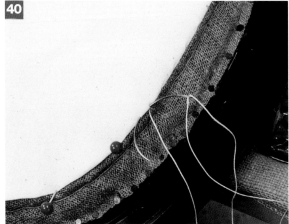

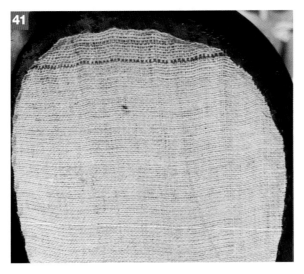

41 The chair back is lined with a 10oz (280g) hessian and then covered with a layer of skin wadding in preparation for the calico covering.

42 The completed chair.

8 Gallery

Y ou will find in this gallery a selection of upholstered pieces that include a satisfying combination of the technical and the creative. A great deal of pleasure can be gained from the restoring and rebuilding of much-loved chairs, stools and ottomans. The range here offers inspiration for ways to renovate and update and will provide ideas for adding your own stylistic flourishes with fabrics and trimmings.

Our gallery illustrates this wide-ranging subject with a look at the historic and the modern, and an appreciation of the upholsterer's craft.

1 Queen Elizabeth II coronation stool dated 1953

This coronation stool has been restored and reupholstered using most of the original materials. The new fabric and braid is matched exactly to the colours of the original piece. Stamped and made by Waring and Gillow for the coronation of Queen Elizabeth II.

2 French armchair, tapestry cover

A painted French armchair made and upholstered in France. The original handmade tapestry is finished with close nailing.

3 Mid-Victorian ottoman box

An original mid-Victorian ottoman with hinged lid and storage. A walnut plinth hides the brass castors. Upholstered in cotton chenille and hand-stitched trimming.

4 Prince of Wales investiture chair dated 1969

One of 4,000 chairs made for the investiture of the Prince of Wales, these chairs were designed by Lord Snowdon and used at Caernarfon Castle for the investiture ceremony. Stamped and dated and restored using the original red wool fabric.

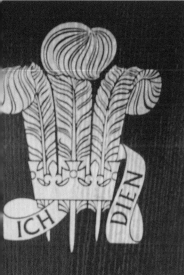

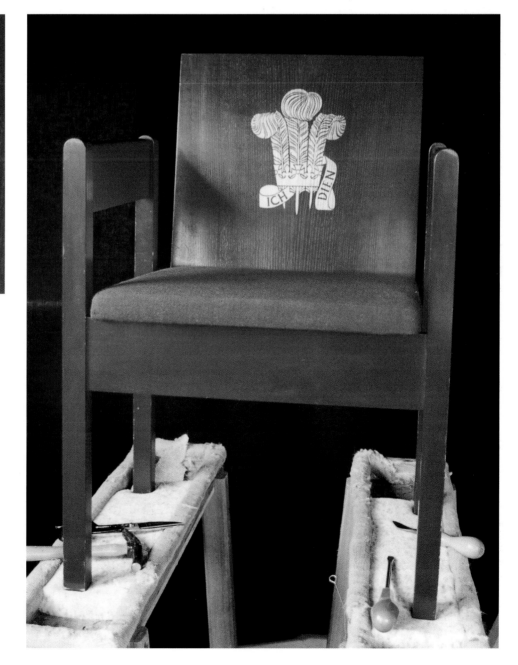

5 Painted French armchair, embroidered

A painted beechwood armchair,
part of a three-piece suite, restored
and completely reupholstered in an
embroidered charcoal cotton/polyester.
The upholstery is finished with double
piping along all edges.

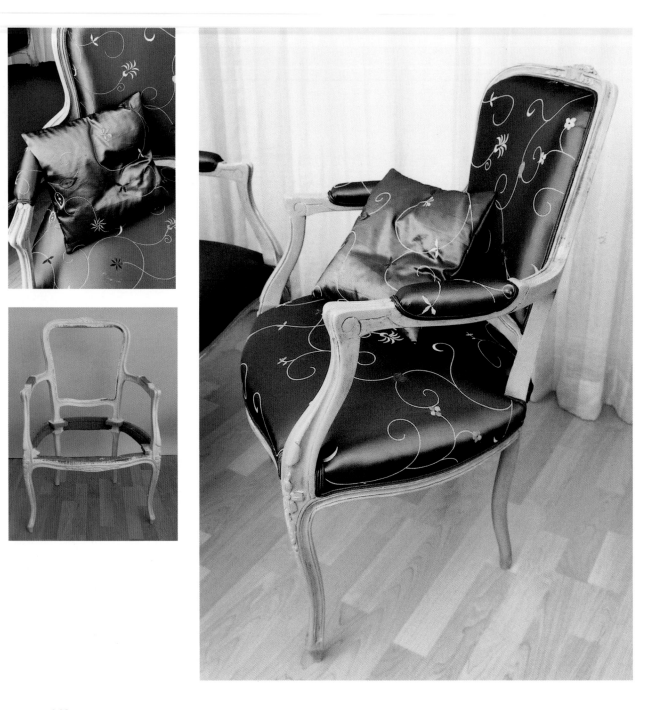

6 Edwardian dining chairs, pierced carving

A set of Edwardian dining chairs with interesting carved and pierced mahogany backrests and marquetry ovals. Carefully restored and reupholstered, the seats remain unsprung.

7 Victorian child's chair, fluted iron back

A mid-Victorian fluted-back child's chair. The chair has an iron back frame and a birch seat frame supported on turned walnut feet. It measures 55cm (22in) in height.

8 Desk armchair c1940

A bent wood desk chair made from
beech with a curving seat and
cruciform underframe. Made in
High Wycombe in about 1940 and
restored in a red cotton chenille
with spaced nailing.

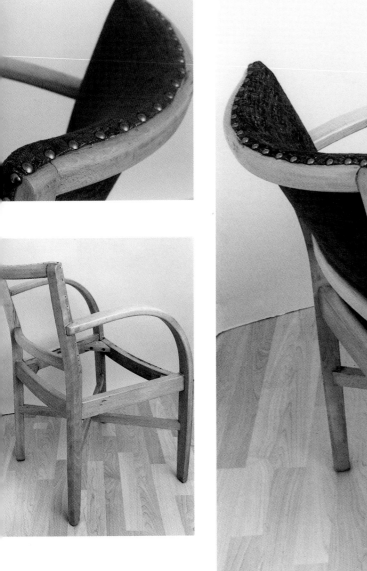

9 Mid-Victorian gilded nursing chair

A mid-Victorian gilded nursing chair on solid brass castors. The seat is sprung and upholstered with a buttoned border, finished with cord and braid.

10 Pair of Biedermeier side chairs

A pair of European side chairs in the Biedermeier style with brass mount decoration and veneered back rails. The seats are unsprung and are covered in cotton tapestry, finished with double piping and brass nails.

11 Pair of Victorian balloon-back chairs

A pair of mid-19th-century walnut balloon-back, parlour chairs, a chair design which was produced over several decades during the Victorian era. There were many variations on cabriole and turned legs. The upholstery is unsprung and covered in a modern damask, trimmed with scroll gimp.

12 French salon chair, late 19th century caned

One of a pair of French parlour chairs carved and painted with caned seat and back supports. The upholstery pads are hand stitched and tied onto the chair with ribbons. Made in the late 19th century, the fluted and carved legs are particularly fine.

13 Louis XVI-style armchair

A modern version of a typical French drawing room chair, in the Directoire style. Upholstered with a traditional sprung platform seat supporting a feather- and down-filled cushion.

14 Pair of Arts and Crafts side chairs

A pair of typically Edwardian Arts
and Crafts period chairs, made
from mahogany with pad feet.
The seats are pinstuffed and
upholstered in a jacquard chenille.

15 Late Victorian mahogany foot stool, tapestry

An attractive 19th-century foot stool
with a drop-in seat, upholstered in
a hand-stitched tapestry, tailor-
made for the stool. The stool has
ball and claw cabriole feet.

16 Late Victorian window seat, one of a pair

One of a pair of late Victorian window or corner seats, fully upholstered with sprung seat and back rest. The turned legs are made in mahogany and are supported on brass and china castors. The seat is upholstered in a chenille tapestry and trimmed with upholstery cord.

17 Pair of oak kneelers, with tapestry

A pair of oak church kneelers or prayer stools, restored and reupholstered in new tapestries, hand stitched to fit the stools. The upholstery sits on solid oak boards and is finished with a fine braid.

18 Early 20th-century tub chair

An early 20th-century tub chair
upholstered in a modern damask
using traditional materials. The back
is trimmed with piping and the arm
facings with a matching cord.

19 Bergere settee, caned with squab

A late Victorian bergere settee
with caned seat, back and arms.
An attractive two-seater on fluted
and carved legs, the seat is
upholstered with a hair-filled squab
trimmed with velvet piping.

20 Round stool, cherry wood, modern

A modern round foot stool on cherry wood legs with a natural polish. Upholstered in a honey-coloured chenille, the stool is trimmed with a large piping and spaced brass nailing.

21 Early Victorian piano stool, adjustable

An early 19th-century walnut music
stool with adjustable seat. The turned
column and base is supported on
carved feet. A reclaimed handmade
tapestry on the seat is bordered with
cotton suede and trimmed with cord
and braid.

22 An Edwardian Hepplewhite-style inlaid mahogany settee

An Edwardian Hepplewhite-style
mahogany settee, with a top-
stuffed seat upholstered in a velour
stripe and trimmed with an
Oxford braid.

23 French folding stool

A turned and ebonized French folding
stool. The seat has a canvas base
and is covered with a linen print,
trimmed with a pom pom fringe.

24 Painted and gilded armchair

A recently made French armchair, painted and gilded and covered in a handmade tapestry. The chair has a modern tension-sprung seat and is finished with traditional antique brass nailing.

25 George III hoop-back side chair

A late 18th-century mahogany hoop-back chair.
The curving seat and the hoop back is typical of the
Hepplewhite style of 1780. A mahogany shoe sits at
the back of the seat to cover and finish the upholstery.
The seat is tufted in the 18th-century style.

26 French upright armchair, pair

One of a pair of walnut, French drawing room chairs, with ribbon carvings along the top of the back. All four legs of the chair are turned and fluted, and the arms are heavily carved, typical of the late 19th-century French style.

27 Caned armchair early 20th century, pair

One of a pair of 1930s caned armchairs with shallow upholstered seats covered in a handmade wool tapestry. The frame is beech with a veneered back splat.

Useful addresses

Association of Master Upholsterers and Soft Furnishers
Francis Vaughan House
102 Commercial Street,
Newport, Cardiff NP9 1LU, UK
www. upholsterers.co.uk

British Antique Furniture Restorers' Association (BAFRA)
The Old Rectory
Warmwell, Dorchester,
Dorset DT7 8HQ, UK
www.bafra.org.uk

British Furniture Manufacturers' Association
30 Harcourt Street
London W1H 2AA, UK

Buckinghamshire Chilterns University College
Design Faculty
Queen Alexandra Road
High Wycombe,
Bucks HP11 2JZ, UK
www.bcuc.ac.uk

Chambre d'Apprentissage
Des Industiries de 1'Amb
200 Bis Boulevard Voltaire
75 011 Paris, France

City and Guilds of London Institute
76 Portland Place
London W1N 4AA, UK
www.city-and-guilds.co.uk

The Countryside Agency
John Dower House
Crescent Place, Cheltenham
Gloucestershire GL50 3RA, UK
www.infoville.org.uk

The Crafts Council
44a Pentonville Road, Islington
London N1 9BY, UK
www.craftscouncil.org.uk

Department of Trade and Industry
Ashdown House
123 Victoria Street,
London SW1E 6RB, UK
www.dtiinfo1.dti.gov.uk

Design Council
28 Haymarket
London SW1Y 4SU, UK
www.design-council.org.uk

Furniture, Furnishings and Interiors National Training Organisation (FFINTO)
67 Wollaton Road, Beeston
Nottingham NG9 2NG, UK

Furniture Industry Research Association
Maxwell Road
Stevenage SG1 2EW, UK
www.pws.co.uk

Geffrye Museum
Kingsland Road
London E2 8EA, UK
www.geffrye-museum.org.uk

Guild of Traditional Upholsterers
The Secretary
Cherry Garth, The Hamlet
Gallowstree Common
Reading RG4 9BU, UK
www.gtu.org.uk/

London Metropolitan University
41–71 Commercial Road
London E1 1LA, UK
www.londonmet.ac.uk

The National Council for Vocational Qualifications
222 Euston Road
London NW1 2BZ, UK
www.qca.org.uk

National Trust
36 Queen Anne's Gate
London SW1H 9AS, UK
www.nationaltrust.org.uk

Upholstery Design and Management Magazine
Published by Chartwell
Communications
Illinois USA
www.udmonline.com

Victoria and Albert Museum
South Kensington
London SW7 2RL, UK
www.vam.ac.uk

Table of UK/USA upholstery terms

UK TERMS	USA TERMS
Roll or piece	Bolt of fabric
Loose seat	Slip seat
Cutting plan	Cutting chart
Border	Boxing strip
Fibre	Moss
Hessian	Burlap
Wadding	Batting
Calico	Muslin
Edge roll	Stuffed roll
Piping cord	Welt cord
Zig-zag	No-sag
Dished seat	Sag seat
Spring unit	Marshall unit
Back spring	Pillow spring
Lashed	Tied
Regulator	Stuffing skewer
Gimp pins	Gimp tacks
Valences	Flounces
Stool	Ottoman
Loose cover	Slip cover
Ruching	Gathering
Tub chair	Barrel chair
Ruche	Loop fringe
Fluting	Channeling
Buttoning	Tufting
Wool felt	Excelsior
Bottoming	Cambric
Ripping chisel	Tack puller
Dug roll	Frame edging
Platform	Seat front
Slip stitching	Blind stitching
Back tacking	Blind tacking
Double-cone springs	Coil springs
Fly	Stretcher
Double piping	Double cording
Close nailing	Nail trim

Glossary

When buying upholstery materials and discussing the work that you are doing with other upholsterers, being familiar with the language of the craft and its technical terms is essential. Many of the terms are historic and have been used over the last 300 years to describe the techniques and materials used by craftsmen, from the early upholders of the 17th century to today's traditional upholsterers and upholstery.

ADHESIVE a contact glue used to fix and hold in place fabrics, foams and trimmings. May be applied by tube, gun or sprayed.

ALVA MARINA a traditional seaweed stuffing often to be found in chairs made at the end of the 19th century and early 20th century. Mainly used as a first stuffing.

ANTIQUE NAILS decorative nails made from brass or brass on steel with a plain or decorative dome head. Very fashionable in the 18th century in Europe and America and still used today with leather coverings.

BACKSTITCH used to produce strong handsewn seams, giving the appearance of a large machine-sewn seam, with each stitch linked to its neighbour.

BIAS CUT the diagonal line or cut that crosses a fabric at a 45 degree angle. Often used in upholstery in scrim work and in the making of pipings.

BLANKET STITCH a handsewn stitch along the edge of fabrics such as scrim and hessian. Used as a feather-edge stitch in early Victorian upholstery.

BLIND STITCH a stitch used to create a firm foundation in the building of stitched-edge upholstery. Two or three rows of blind stitching will produce a very firm edge. (USA see SLIP STITCH)

BOLSTER a cylindrical-shaped cushion used as a support on sofas and chaise longues. Bolsters are sometimes decorated with cording and tassels or may be kept plain with piped seams.

BOXED CUSHION also described as a bordered cushion. A chair back or seat cushion with bordered edges, sewn into a boxed shape with plain or piped seams.

BRADAWL a sharp pointed tool with a wooden handle used to make pilot holes in timber framing.

BROCADE a fabric with a delicate and colourful woven pattern made on a jacquard loom. A traditional upholstery fabric.

BUTTON MOULDS the metal parts of an upholstery button which are fabric covered to a range of different sizes from ⅜in (1cm) up to 2in (5cm) diameter.

CAMPAIGN CHAIR may be a folding chair or a demountable chair which can be transported easily and easily reassembled, typically mid-19th century.

CAPON a pre-made or tailored fabric covering which can be pulled onto a part of a chair, such as an arm or a wing.

CHAMFER to cut and remove the edge of solid materials such as timber, at 45 degrees. For example, seat rail edges are chamfered in preparation for tacking.

CHIPFOAM often called reconstituted foam or 'recon', made up from foam waste and refoamed to produce a very dense upholstery filling.

CLAW HAMMER a tacking hammer with a face at one end and a claw at the other. Can be used to lift out tacks and nails.

CLOSE NAILING decorative upholstery nails set close along an edge to close and finish the upholstery covering.

COIR a fibre from the coconut husk which is cleaned and curled and used as a first stuffing particularly over sprung foundations. May be natural ginger colour or dyed black.

CORD an upholstery trimming made in the form of rope from gimped yarns, and often in various colours, used to decorate or finish an edge. Some cords are flanged to make application easier.

CORDING NEEDLE a small 2in (5cm) or 2⅜in(6cm) curved needle used to close fabrics and sew on cord to an edge.

COTTON FELT a relatively modern filling made from cotton linters and felted into sheet form, used as a topping over second stuffings.

CUTS making the cuts in an upholstered chair to allow the fabric to fit around the frame uprights. For example, 'V' cuts and straight cuts.

CUTTING PLAN a sketch or drawn plan of the fabric parts to be cut from a length of upholstery fabric. Sizes can be added and the total amount of fabric required can be calculated.

DEEP BUTTONING often called diamond buttoning. The upholstery fabric is pulled deeply into the filling with a button and twine to form a design using several buttons arranged in a diamond formation.

DOUBLE CONE SPRINGS often referred to as waisted or hourglass, these springs are used in traditional seating and sewn onto webbings.

DOUBLE-ENDED NEEDLE a two-point needle used to produce stitched edges and stuffing ties, etc. The needle points may be round or bayonette.

DOUBLE PIPING a trimming which is made on the sewing machine using a strip of fabric 2¾in (7cm) wide and two rows of piping cord. May be glued or stapled in place.

DROP ARM an adjustable arm on a settee, typical of a Chesterfield or Knole settee.

DROP-IN SEAT a seat or back frame which is upholstered and then fitted into a chair with show-wood surrounds.

ENGLISH WEBBING a traditional upholstery webbing with black and white yarns made with a twill herringbone weave. Also made with undyed yarns which are brown and white.

ESTIMATING calculating quantities and costs so that an estimate can be produced before work begins.

FIBRE upholstery fillings which are vegetable, in the form of grasses or nut fibres.

FINE TACKS tacks with small heads available in all leg lengths. Ideal for temporary tacking and the fixing of scrims, calico and fabrics.

FIRST STUFFING the base stuffing in a chair, which may be fibre or hair and held in place with bridles and ties.

FLANGED CORD an upholstery cord with a narrow tape sewn along its edge to facilitate fixing.

FLAX TWINE a fine smooth mattress twine in various thicknesses, ideal for all types of stitch work.

FLOCK rag flock and wool flock are traditional fillings made from waste textile fibres. Used today as pre-formed felts and pads.

FLUTING created by stuffing separate channels using upholstery fabric, machine or hand-sewn, usually in chair backs.

FLY PIECE strips of fabric added to the edges of the main parts of a chair cover to extend them at tuckaways and reduce costs.

FOAM upholstery foams are mainly produced from polyurethane and some latex qualities. Can be cut or moulded for use as a filling.

FRAME the supporting structure or skeleton of a chair or settee.

FRINGE a decorative trimming used in upholstery since the early 17th century.

GATHERED used on chair borders, skirts and valences to produce fullness and effect in a fabric.

G-CRAMP an adjustable cramp in the shape of a 'G' used to hold materials tightly together during assembly.

GIMP PIN available in many colours, these fine tacks have small heads and are used to finish fabrics and trimmings.

GLUE GUN a tool used to heat up and apply hot adhesive, for bonding porous materials.

HAIR horse, pig, cow and goat hair is used as a high-quality upholstery filling in traditional upholstery.

HALF HITCH a knot used regularly in upholstery to tie springs and finish off a line of stitching. Two half hitches will seal and finish a twine end.

HIDE the seasoned and tanned skins of animals such as cow, sheep, goat and pig. used as coverings for upholstered chairs.

IMPROVED TACKS upholstery tacks with large heads used for fixing webbings, hessians and tarpaulins.

INSIDE ARM the inner surface covering running from the seat level up and over the arm of a chair.

INSIDE BACK the surface covering of the back-rest part of a chair.

INTERLINING a soft woven cream-coloured blanket-like fabric used as an inner lining, in curtains, wall coverings and screens, called bump.

JACQUARD a weaving system used to produce patterns in fabrics.

JUTE an Indian vegetable fibre used in the manufacture of webbings, hessians, scrims and tarpaulins.

LASHING the technique of tying and knotting springs with laid cord to hold them in place.

LEATHER a tanned, dyed and finished hide.

LINEN a textile fibre made from raw flax, often blended with cotton.

MAGNETIC HAMMER a tacking hammer with a magnetic face used to pick up tacks.

MALLET a wooden hammer usually made from beech used to tap the ripping chisel when removing tacks.

MOUQUETTE a hardwearing upholstery fabric with a pile surface which may be looped or cut.

NOTCH a 'V' cut from the edge of a fabric which is used as a centre mark or to match up during cutting and sewing.

OUTSIDE ARM the arm covering on the outside of a chair arm.

OUTSIDE BACK the outer surface covering at the back of a chair.

OUTSIDE WING the outer covering fabric on the wing of a wing armchair.

PASSEMENTERIE the French term used to describe all kinds of trimmings and decoration in furnishing.

PILE FABRIC those woven fabrics with a surface pile, for example, velour, velvet, corduroy.

PINCERS the tool used to lift out nails and tacks from wood surfaces.

PIPING FOOT a sewing machine presser foot with a grooved sole, designed specifically for making piping.

PLATFORM the seat in a chair which is upholstered in preparation for supporting a fitted cushion.

POLYESTER FIBRE a soft white wadding made in several weights and thicknesses. Also produced in loose form as a cushion filling. Used most successfully as a wrap under upholstery fabric.

PULL-IN a channel produced in a chair back by deep stitching giving shape and form to a surface. A French technique.

RAILS the main timber parts of a chair frame.

RASP a tool used to remove the sharp edges on timber frames and produce chamfers prior to tacking down scrim.

REBATE a recess cut into timber rails in order to house fixed or drop-in upholstery.

REGULATOR an upholstery tool made from steel with a sharp point and a flat end; the regulator has many uses, particularly the regulating and moving of stuffings.

RIPPER a ripping chisel used to remove tacks and staples, may be straight blade or cranked.

ROLL EDGE a shaped edge in the form of a roll of stuffing held down with scrim or calico and tacked in place.

ROSETTE a circular trimming created with a fabric, a cord or a gimped yarn, used on its own or with a tassel.

RUBBERIZED HAIR a sheet filling material made from animal hair bonded with natural and synthetic rubbers, usually 1in (2.5cm) thick.

SCRIM a loosely woven fabric made from linen or jute, used to mould the first stuffing and the stitched edges in good-quality upholstery.

SEAM ALLOWANCE the ⅜in (1cm) or ½in (1.3cm) margin allowed when two fabrics are being machine sewn.

SECOND STUFFING the soft layer of filling tied in over scrim before the calico covering. Usually curled hair or wool felt.

SELF-PIPING a single piping made up from the upholstery fabric, usually bias cut.

SHOW-WOOD the visible polished or painted surface on a chair frame.

SKEWERS long upholstery pins used to secure materials prior to sewing. The most common lengths used are 3in and 4in (7.5cm and 10cm).

SLIP STITCH a hand made closing seam using waxed linen thread and a curved needle.

SPRING CANVAS a heavyweight hessian 14oz and above, known as tarpaulin, and used over spring foundations.

SPRING NEEDLE a 5in (12.5cm) curved needle used to tie springs in place onto webbing bases.

SQUAB a slim cushion pad filled with curled hair, wool fleece or feathers, mainly in seating.

STOCKINETTE a lightweight knitted fabric made from cotton or polyester and used over foam and fibre interiors.

STUFFING TIES deep ties made with twine to hold a first stuffing in place.

TACK ROLL often called a dug roll. The firm edge made with hessian or scrim and a core filling of hair, fibre or felt.

TACKS the traditional upholstery fixing available in fine and improved qualities and various lengths.

TAILORS' CHALK used for marking out fabrics and linings, available in several colours.

TAPESTRY a handmade or machine-made fabric of good weight and traditionally used as a decorative covering for seating.

TEASE the technique used to open up and separate fibre and hair stuffing to produce a fine soft surface.

TEMPORARY TACK tacks which are used to set the position of materials on a chair frame and are only hammered half into the timber; can be removed quickly.

TOP STITCH a knotted edge stitch produced with a two-point needle to create a firm sharp edge line.

TUFTS may be functional or decorative and in the form of a small floret of wool or silk. Used in upholstery and mattress making to contain and hold stuffed components; an early form of buttoning.

TUCKAWAY fabrics and linings pushed out of sight at the point where inside backs and inside arms meet a seat.

WADDING a fine cotton filling known as skin wadding and used over second stuffings and over calico to hold back other fibrous fillings.

WARP the threads or yarns which run the length of a fabric.

WEFT the threads or yarns which run across the width of a woven fabric.

Index

Acknowledgements

A very sincere thank you to all of the following without whom, this book would not have been possible.

Vitafoam UK
Gutermann UK
A and C Valmic
Isaac Lord
The late Mrs L Afshar
Maureen Batey

Ifte Wangsa
Mr and Mrs Cliff Gill
Mr and Mrs M Afshar
Elham Gaffari
Fred Caulfield-Kerney
Angela Burgin
Mr and Mrs H Nasr
Peter Legg
Farideh Ziaian
Mr and Mrs K Afshar
Mr and Mrs M V Afshar

Janet Wilkinson
Pyrton Village Church, Oxford
Buckinghamshire Chilterns
University College, Design
Faculty

My editor Clare Miller for her tremendous support, and the Guild of Master Craftsman Publications.

Titles available from
GMC Publications

Books

Woodturning

Bowl Turning Techniques Masterclass	*Tony Boase*
Chris Child's Projects for Woodturners	*Chris Child*
Decorating Turned Wood: The Maker's Eye	
	Liz & Michael O'Donnell
Green Woodwork	*Mike Abbott*
A Guide to Work-Holding on the Lathe	*Fred Holder*
Keith Rowley's Woodturning Projects	*Keith Rowley*
Making Screw Threads in Wood	*Fred Holder*
Segmented Turning: A Complete Guide	*Ron Hampton*
Turned Boxes: 50 Designs	*Chris Stott*
Turning Green Wood	*Michael O'Donnell*
Turning Pens and Pencils	*Kip Christensen & Rex Burningham*
Wood for Woodturners	*Mark Baker*
Woodturning: Forms and Materials	*John Hunnex*
Woodturning: A Foundation Course (New Edition)	*Keith Rowley*
Woodturning: A Fresh Approach	*Robert Chapman*
Woodturning: An Individual Approach	*Dave Regester*
Woodturning: A Source Book of Shapes	*John Hunnex*
Woodturning Masterclass	*Tony Boase*
Woodturning Projects: A Workshop Guide to Shapes	*Mark Baker*

Woodworking

Beginning Picture Marquetry	*Lawrence Threadgold*
Carcass Furniture	*GMC Publications*
Celtic Carved Lovespoons: 30 Patterns	
	Sharon Littley & Clive Griffin
Celtic Woodcraft	*Glenda Bennett*
Celtic Woodworking Projects	*Glenda Bennett*
Complete Woodfinishing (Revised Edition)	*Ian Hosker*
David Charlesworth's Furniture-Making Techniques	
	David Charlesworth
David Charlesworth's Furniture-Making Techniques – Volume 2	*David Charlesworth*
Furniture Projects with the Router	*Kevin Ley*
Furniture Restoration (Practical Crafts)	*Kevin Jan Bonner*
Furniture Restoration: A Professional at Work	*John Lloyd*
Furniture Workshop	*Kevin Ley*
Green Woodwork	*Mike Abbott*
History of Furniture: Ancient to 1900	*Michael Huntley*

Intarsia: 30 Patterns for the Scrollsaw	*John Everett*
Making Heirloom Boxes	*Peter Lloyd*
Making Screw Threads in Wood	*Fred Holder*
Making Woodwork Aids and Devices	*Robert Wearing*
Mastering the Router	*Ron Fox*
Pine Furniture Projects for the Home	*Dave Mackenzie*
Router Magic: Jigs, Fixtures and Tricks to Unleash your Router's Full Potential	*Bill Hylton*
Router Projects for the Home	*GMC Publications*
Router Tips & Techniques	*Robert Wearing*
Routing: A Workshop Handbook	*Anthony Bailey*
Routing for Beginners (Revised and Expanded Edition)	*Anthony Bailey*
Stickmaking: A Complete Course	
	Andrew Jones & Clive George
Stickmaking Handbook	*Andrew Jones & Clive George*
Storage Projects for the Router	*GMC Publications*
Success with Sharpening	*Ralph Laughton*
Veneering: A Complete Course	*Ian Hosker*
Veneering Handbook	*Ian Hosker*
Wood: Identification & Use	*Terry Porter*
Woodworking Techniques and Projects	*Anthony Bailey*
Woodworking with the Router: Professional Router Techniques any Woodworker can Use	
	Bill Hylton & Fred Matlack

Upholstery

Upholstery: A Beginners' Guide	*David James*
Upholstery: A Complete Course (Revised Edition)	*David James*
Upholstery Restoration	*David James*
Upholstery Techniques & Projects	*David James*
Upholstery Tips and Hints	*David James*

magazines

Woodturning • Woodcarving
Furniture & Cabinetmaking
The Router • New Woodworking
The Dolls' House Magazine
Outdoor Photography
Black & White Photography
Knitting • Guild News

The above represents a selection of titles currently published or scheduled to be published. All are available direct from the Publishers or through bookshops, newsagents and specialist retailers. To place an order, or to obtain a complete catalogue, contact:

GMC Publications,
166 High Street, Lewes, East Sussex BN7 1XU United Kingdom
Tel: 01273 488005 Fax: 01273 402866
E-mail: pubs@thegmcgroup.com Website: www.gmcbooks.com
Orders by credit card are accepted